Vaastu Corrections *without* Demolitions

Vaastu Corrections *without* Demolitions

By

A.R. Hari

Administrative office and sale centre

J-3/16 , Daryaganj, New Delhi-110002
☎ 23276539, 23272783, 23272784 • *Fax:* 011-23260518
E-mail: info@pustakmahal.com • *Website:* www.pustakmahal.com

Branches
Bengaluru: ☎ 080-22234025 • *Telefax:* 080-22240209
E-mail: pustakmahalblr@gmail.com
Mumbai: ☎ 022-22010941, 022-22053387
E-mail: unicornbooksmumbai@gmail.com
Patna: ☎ 0612-3294193 • *Telefax:* 0612-2302719
E-mail: rapidexptn@gmail.com

ISBN 978-81-223-0633-2

Edition: 2016

Price : ₹ 120/-

Printed at : AR Emm International, Delhi

Preface

Man has always sought various ways of solving a problem. This attitude of refusing to accept that there can be only one solution to any problem has given rise to various schools of thoughts in all branches of science and philosophy.

For example medicine offers a host of systems, each with their own merits and shortcomings. However all the systems are thriving thanks to the ingenuity of the founders of these systems and the ever-curious mind of the people who are ready to give it a try.

Vaastu cannot be an exception to this rule. The human mind has always wondered whether corrections are possible without resorting to demolition and rebuilding.

This book is in answer to these questions.

As usual your feedback can help me improvise on my findings.

— Author

Contents

1

What is Vaastu? How does it work?

Vaastu is a science which deals with the creation of a harmonious energy field in a structure. It has nothing to do with religion, rituals or astrology. Making Vaastu a part of these subjects can only do injustice to this science. It is basically a science of structures and to derive the benefits from it and to appreciate it, it is necessary to treat the subject as a pure science. Diluting the subject with superstition in whichever manner can only harm the growth of this science and deny the spread of this valuable knowledge far and wide.

In the last five years or so Vaastu has become a household name in India. It is difficult to find an architect or a builder today in India who has not heard of Vaastu. Such is the popularity of the subject that architects no longer shun clients who are desirous of building houses or offices as per Vaastu. One can confidently say that Vaastu has taken firm roots in India.

Not that the critics of the subject are silent. If any, their voices have grown shriller. They accuse the 'Vaastu pundits' of taking advantage of the gullibility of the masses. I recently read a report that an astro-scientist while criticising Vaastu had offered to stay in any defective building to prove that it could not affect him. Another architect complained loudly that Vaastu pundits were arresting the growth of young architects from exhibiting their ideas and talent.

These are extreme positions. Fortunately no one takes them seriously. And rightly so. If one has to be taken seriously one has to adopt a scientific approach to disprove a statement. For that the following steps are necessary:-

a) Understanding the concept

b) Extensive verification studies

c) Conclusions based on statistics

That is the accepted scientific route. But the critics never followed this method and completely relied on their shrill voices only. Justifiably the public have rejected them outright.

One should not try to force one's views on somebody only because one holds a position of authority. Neither should one criticize a subject or a concept because of one's own prejudices. These people cannot be taken as scientifically tempered. They should be just ignored.

Proving Vaastu as a subject without foundation is not at all a difficult task for the gentlemen who want to do just that. All they have to do is to come out with a list of at least twenty five buildings which do not follow the rules of Vaastu but where the occupants or users of the building are happy, healthy and prosperous over several decades and another twenty five buildings which are conforming to Vaastu but are witness to great familial problems. If they can publish their findings and can establish that the results are indeed contrary to what Vaastu claims to achieve, then the subject of Vaastu will really disappear once and for all. A study of this type is truly scientific and those who complain about Vaastu will have to necessarily undertake this study before proclaiming that it is not a science.

I believe the subject is a science and that it holds tremendous potential to enrich our lives. I have kept an open mind on the subject and my studies show that here indeed is a science which is consistent with results. I, therefore, recommend this wholeheartedly for one and all.

Before we proceed further we will briefly run through the methodology of Vaastu. We have to first know how it works. Only then understand we can how the defects come in the way of getting Vaastu benefits.

Basically Vaastu is all about the interaction of various forms of energy in a structure. As you are aware the whole universe is one expanding mass formed at the time of the big bang. The expansion still goes on churning out more and more galaxies and star systems. From all these astral bodies various types of radiations are being emitted. All radiations are again a form of energy. Although we classify various forms of energy as heat, light, magnetic, electric etc. each can be converted to other and hence all forms of energy are fundamentally the same. There are some forms of energy which we can see or feel like ordinary light and sound. As our senses operate in a limited spectrum, we do not perceive the other forms of energy like ultraviolet rays or infrared rays or supersonic sounds, but they are as much real as the other forms we perceive. As matter is also condensed form of energy, we can easily see that all we perceive as matter or energy is in fact energy only. Thus we ourselves are a part of this energy field.

In Nature the conversion of one form of energy to other is a continuous process. For example, the sun's energy is absorbed by the plants to prepare the food which is later taken by animals and humans. Thus the light energy of the sun is used by the plants to produce food which is in the form of mechanical energy. When it is consumed by humans and animals it is converted into muscular energy, which helps them to sustain themselves.

Further any form of energy under a set of circumstances produces a sense of comfort or uneasiness in an organism. For example, a cool breeze on a hot day is very pleasant but on a chilly day is quite uncomfortable. A glowing hearth on a chilly night has a soothing and cozy effect, but on a hot day is decidedly uncomfortable.

Music played on an instrument helps a person to relax and ease his tension, but the continuous noise of passing traffic can set the nerves of a person on the edge.

Thus we see that for any energy to have the best effect on a living person it is necessary that it is supplied at a level which the organism cherishes. We loosely term places which have a calming effect on us as 'atmosphere'. Many a time we classify various structures as having 'good' or 'bad' atmosphere. If someone asks us to explain the term 'atmosphere', we may be at a loss for words. It is not the lighting or ventilation. It is not the wall colors or the polished flooring. It is not the painting on the wall or the persian carpet on the floor. It is not the gentle music or the comfortable furniture. Still we understand the term 'atmosphere' and nod our head wisely although we are unable.to explain it.

It is probably instinctive and lies beyond comprehension. It cannot be measured or compared with other entities. But we all know that it exists and varies from place to place.

If you have a pet you will notice how sensitive it is to what we call atmosphere. In your house it searches for a specific place where it will curl to relax. Take it away from that place but it will return again and again to the same place. Dogs and cats are endowed with this instinctive ability to find the right atmosphere. We are certainly not as sensitive as they are but all the same we are affected by the atmosphere of a place to some degree.

Vaastu is basically all about creation of this subtle conducive atmosphere in a structure. You have entered houses where you find the atmosphere pleasant. Automatically you relax and are at your witty best. Your responses are cheerful, careful, sensitive and measured. The house brings cheer to you and you in turn bring cheer to others because you are cheerful. And then there are those gloomy houses, dull classrooms, dark laboratories, stinking offices where you start counting your minutes to get out at the first opportunity. People throng to holy places, sacred temples, sea beaches, waterfalls and lakesides, all because of this 'atmosphere'. Hence we have to concede that every place has an 'atmosphere' which either is positive or negative. While a human being thrives in a positive atmosphere he is bogged down by negative emotions in a 'negative' atmosphere.

A 'positive' atmosphere brings out the best in us. Our mind is calm and relaxed and the body feels healthy and strong. This atmosphere makes us think positively, makes our approaches positive and hence positive results automatically follow. Everyone coming under the influence of this atmosphere feels likewise. A family in such an atmosphere is a happy family and everything in their lives goes so smoothly that we come to the conclusion that they are blessed. Take the family in an 'negative' atmosphere and you find that for no fault of their's they undergo tension and mental torture. The body is tense, prone to illness of one type or other. The mind is tense leading to strained relationships which forms a vicious cycle around them and aggravates all kinds of sufferings.

Thus if we are successful in creating this 'good atmosphere' inside a structure we will succeed in ensuring the health and happiness of the inhabitants.

The same principles apply for a shopping establishment, industry or a business center. In all these places, the workers are cheerful, their approach is positive and the plans are put into faultless execution ensuring an all-round growth of the enterprise.

2

Defects and Their Effects

Any energy is a flow of a field from a higher potential to the lower. This can be mechanical, electrical or cosmic. The laws are the same.

A plot represents both the positive and negative forces in a balanced sphere. This balance gets disturbed when the structure is placed in it. A balance in a plot is achieved when the positive and negative parts of the plot has an equal potential. (fig 1)

Here the north and east portions represent the positive field and the south and west portions represent the negative field. Granting that the level in the plot is uniform we have a well-balanced plot.

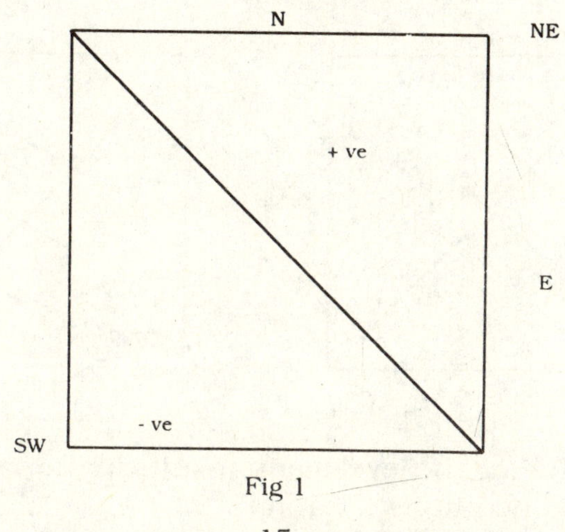

Fig 1

An imbalance between the two fields can be created by the following methods.

1) Increasing the level of any sector weakens that sector
2) Reducing the level by taking away the earth increases the strength of that particular sector
3) Creating extensions increases the area of that particular sector thereby increasing the strength of that particular sector
4) Water bodies enhance the strength of that particular sector

Let us understand these concepts more clearly with the help of figures. See fig (2) and fig (3). In fig. (2), you find that the level of the positive sector is higher in comparison to the negative sector. Because of this the strength of the positive field decreases and the negative increases. In this case energy flows from the negative portion to the positive portion. In essence the plot therefore has, what is known as the 'negative energy' flow.

See the fig (3) where the higher level is in the negative sector. In this case, the energy flows from the positive to negative side and hence the plot has a natural 'positive' energy flow.

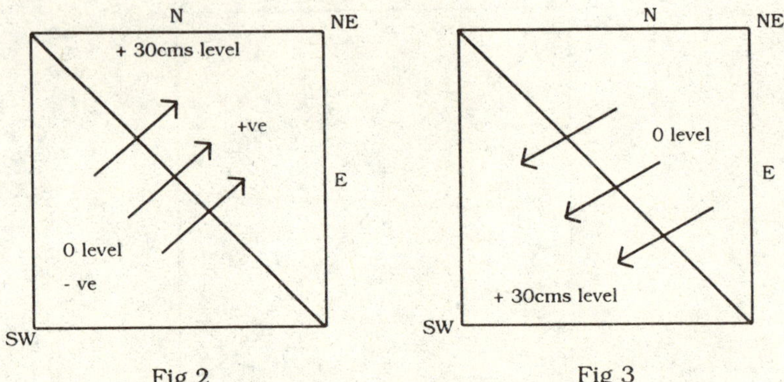

Fig 2   Fig 3

Reducing the level again results in the same impact as explained in fig (2) and (3).

If the plot extends in a positive direction then the area covered by the positive portion increases and provided the level is uniform, the flow of energy takes place from the sector which has the extended corner towards the otherside.

See fig (4). Here the northeast portion is extended. Hence the field area of the positive sector is more. If the level is uniform, the flow takes place from the positive side to the negative resulting in a positive energy plot.

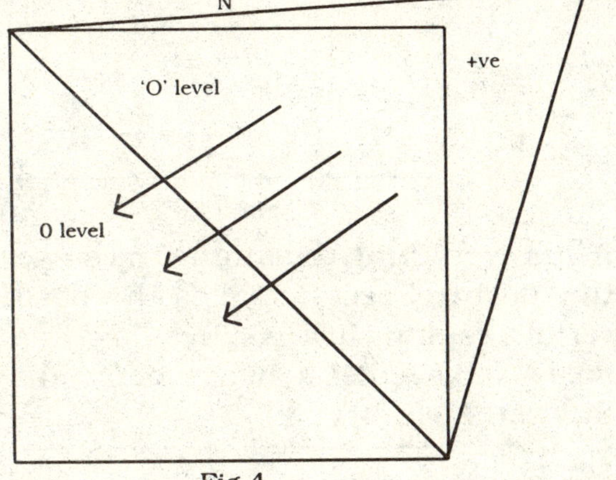

Fig 4

The reverse happens in case the negative portion extends. See fig (5). As the negative sector is more powerful, a negative current flows towards the positive turning the energy flow pattern into 'negative'.

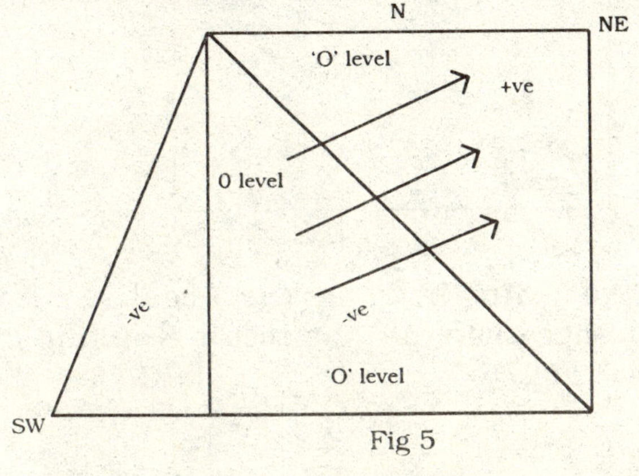

Fig 5

A water body basically represents a depression. Water can collect only when a portion of the land is depressed or is at a lower level. Fig 6(a)

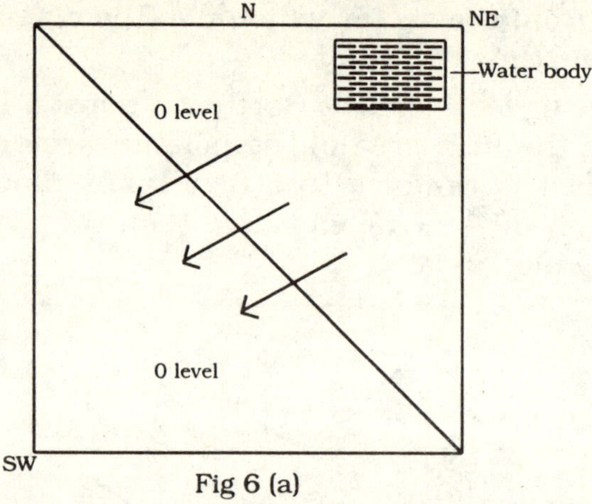

Fig 6 (a)

Thus everything remaining the same, a water body in the 'positive' sector makes the positive half more powerful, resulting in a 'positive' flow. See Fig(6-a) Same effect is achieved if a heavy body like a rock is in southwest. Fig(6-b)

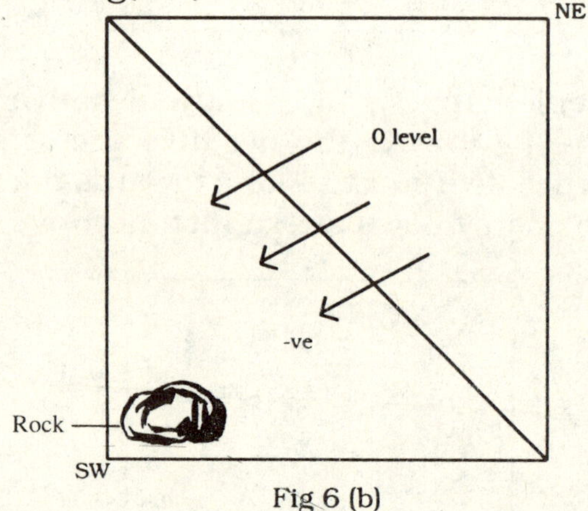

Fig 6 (b)

Similarly a water body in the negative sector increases the negativity of that sector resulting in a 'negative flow'. Fig(7)

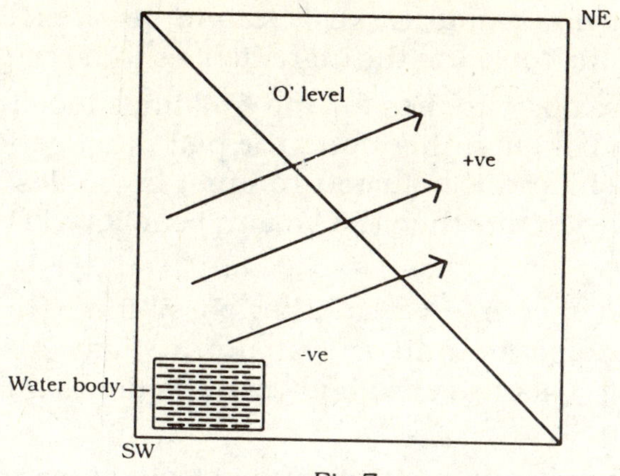

Fig 7

So far we have discussed the positive and negative features of plots. We will now see how the constructional aspects of the building affect the flow.

Vaastu for Buildings

It should be noted that the plot can only generate a positive field if the plot conforms to Vaastu. But the building should be constructed in such a manner that it receives the flow thus generated. So we see that actually there are two aspects in the construction of buildings. One, the plot which should generate a positive field and second, the building which should receive the field inside. Technically therefore it is possible to have a powerful field but a wrong structure could make the complete Vaastu ineffective. Conversely it possible to have a building exactly conforming to Vaastu but on a wrong plot which again nullifies the Vaastu effects.

Take an example. If a tasty dish is to be prepared, you must have an excellent cook, and ingredients of good quality. If you have a bad cook then notwithstanding the fact that the ingredients were of very good quality, you end up with a spoiled dish. Same thing happens if the cook is good but the ingredients are of poor quality. If the dish has to be of excellent taste, both the cook and the ingredients should be good.

Same analogy applies for the buildings too. To get the Vaastu benefits, therefore, the plot must generate a strong field and the structure must be so designed as to receive it. Only then the Vaastu benefits will reach the residents.

There is of course yet another possibility. The plot could be defective and the structure may also be defective. In this case the end result is deprivation of Vaastu benefits.

We will now see how various defects come in the way of the structure receiving the flow in spite of the fact that the plot is generating a positive flow.

See Fig(8). Here the plot is as per Vaastu and the building which is on the ground floor is properly placed to receive the positive energy.

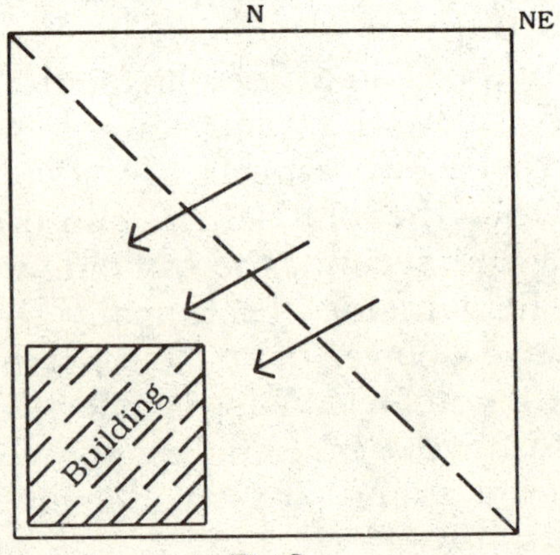

Fig 8

In fig (9) the building covers the positive sector, thereby weakening it and the wrong sectors are opened up, making them stronger. In this case the building receives a negative flow and granting that the building is as per Vaastu, the benefits of Vaastu to the residents do not follow.

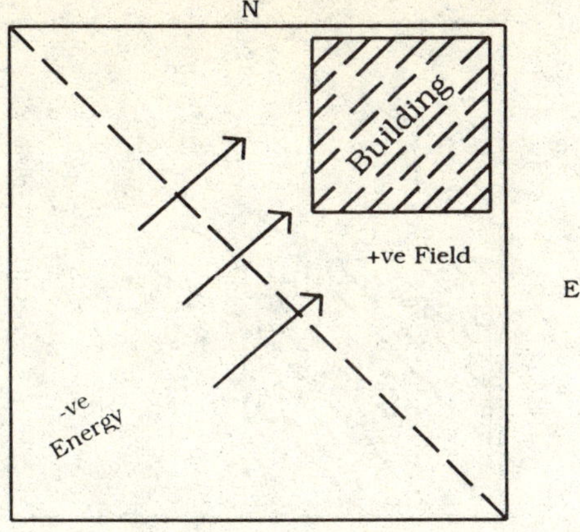

Fig 9

Now let us go back to fig (8) and familiarise ourselves with the various factors which can arrest the positive flow in spite of a strong positive field trying to enter the structure.

Fig (10) shows a building in which the toilet is present in the northeast corner. Defecation and fecal matter arrests the positive flow with the result that the building becomes Vaastu negative.

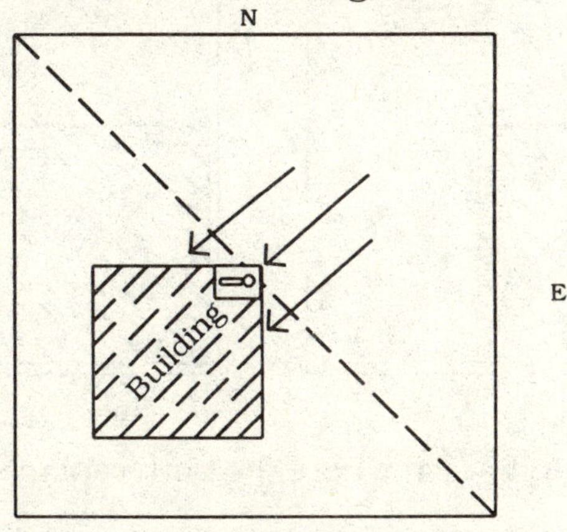

Fig 10

In fig (11) we have a staircase in the northeast corner. Again weight here arrests the flow inside the structure.

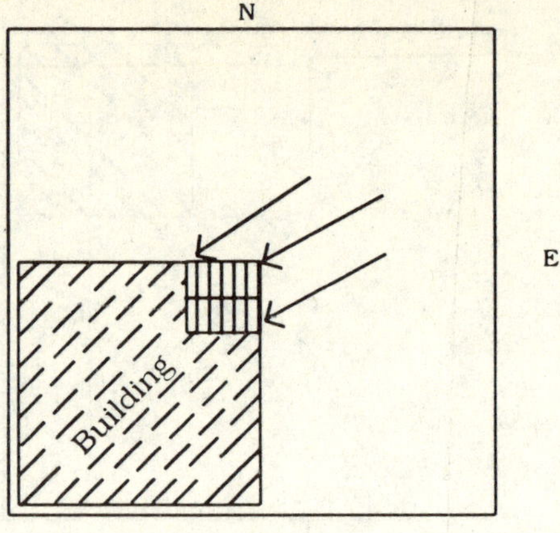

Fig 11

In fig (12), a store closing the northeast corner negates the flow whereas in fig (13), a kitchen comes in the way of the structure receiving the positive current. Heat in this sector virtually nullifies all the positive currents.

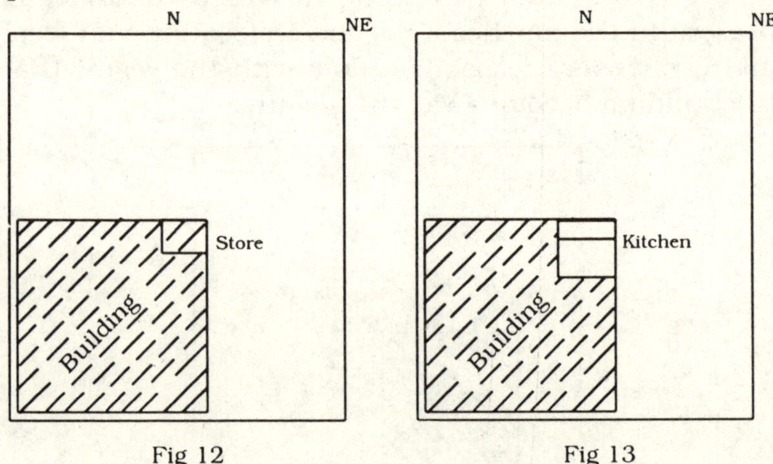

Fig 12

Fig 13

Same in fig (14) where the bath replaces the kitchen.

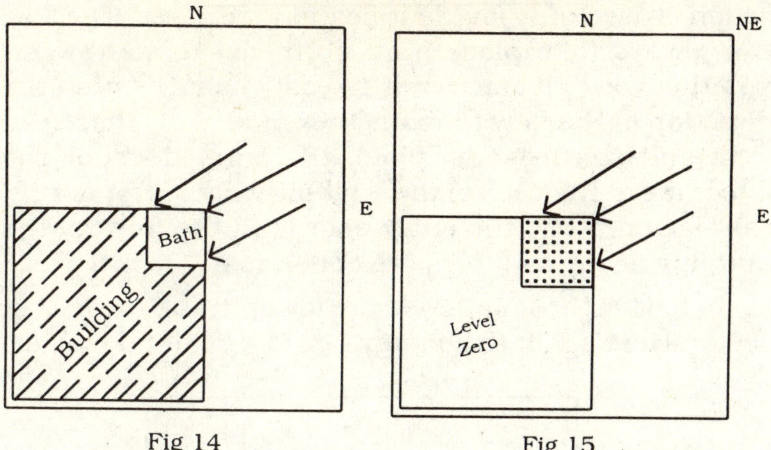

Fig 14 Fig 15

A higher floor level in northeast sector of the building as shown in fig(15) again prevents the flow from taking place. Wrong entry or exit doors in the north-northwest, the south-southwest, the west-southwest and the east-southeast disrupts the flow of energy inside a structure. The effect is more pronounced if they are single doors. The effect gets reduced somewhat if there is another door in the northeast sector of the building. See fig 16.

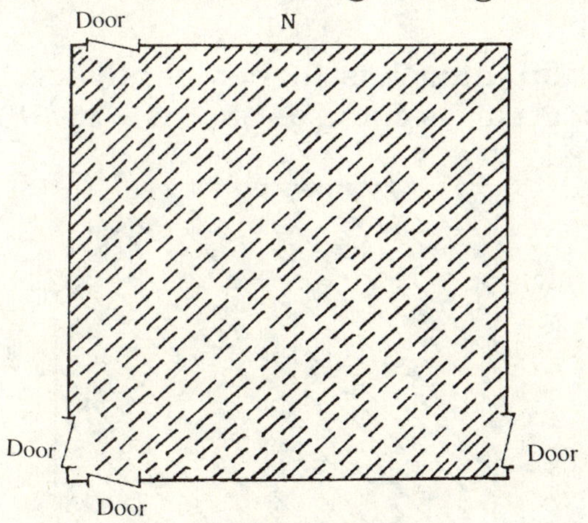

Fig 16

One should note that the terms 'entry' door or 'main' door and 'exit' door or 'back' door are relative terms which is used only for identification purposes. The flow can always take place from northeast to southwest. Whether your plot faces north/east or south/west, the direction of the flow remains the same. Only in case of west and south-facing plots, the entry door for the forces are at the back of the building whereas for north/east-facing plots, the entry door is in the front of the building as far as forces are concerned.

In fig(17) the floor levels are lower in the southwest sector. Here again the energy flow does not take place.

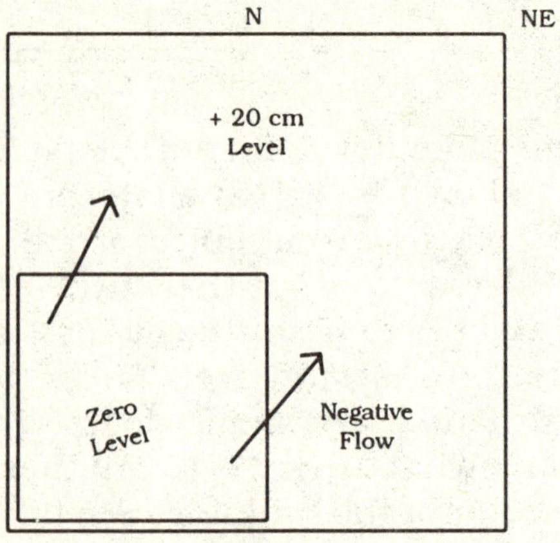

Fig 17

If the building has higher plinth level and the northeast sector is cutoff as shown in fig(18), the flow is distorted.

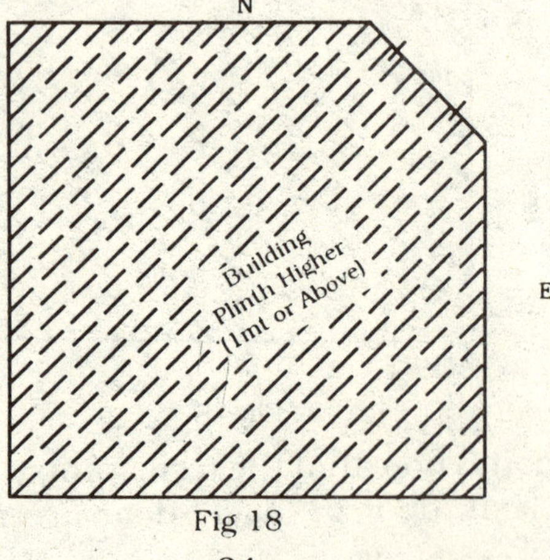

Fig 18

Fig(19) shows the levels and placements of the various utilities inside the structure to get the best vaastu benefits. Here you see that openings are kept in the northeast sector readily allowing the energy to easily enter. A depressed level here sucks the current making a strong field inside.

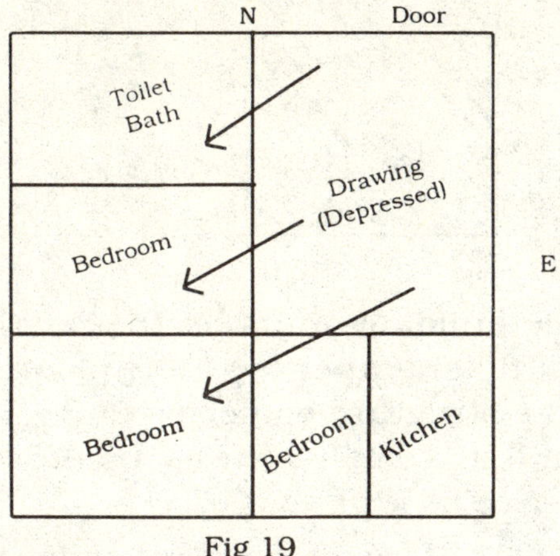

Fig 19

The kitchen in the southeast and toilet and bath in the northwest aid the flow to reach all sectors in full strength. The bedrooms are placed in the southwest, west and the south where abundant reflected bioenergy ensures the health of the members of the family.

We will now see how the first floor and subsequent floors can suffer from Vaastu defects. A first floor has no periphery. Thus the fact that you have a very good northeast current in the ground floor is of no consequence here. The plot of the first floor is the roof of the ground floor. Thus to have good Vaastu benefits we need to provide low level open terraces in the northeast sector so that sufficient energy to sustain the requirement of the first floor building is generated in the open roof area. Necessarily the balconies and open terraces are to come towards the north, east and the northeast.

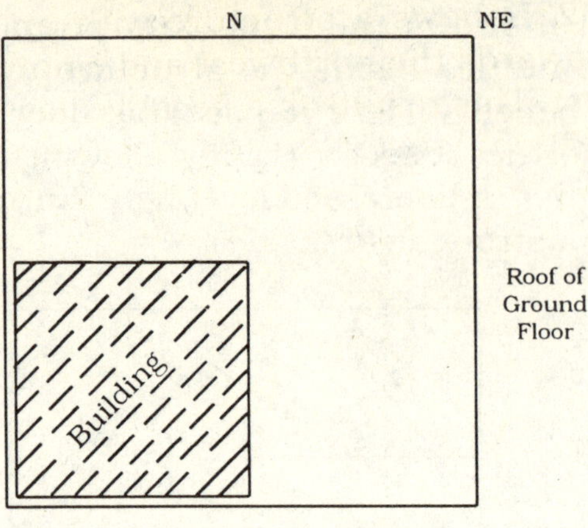

Fig 20

Here the building abuts on the Southwest corner leaving sufficient open space in north and east. Provided the structure conforms to Fig(19) we have a perfect house which abides by Vaastu and its principles. See fig (20)

See fig (21). Here we have balconies in the north-northwest or the west-southwest or the south-southwest or east-southeast. If there are no balancing balconies in the northeast sector, then the house has defective Vaastu.

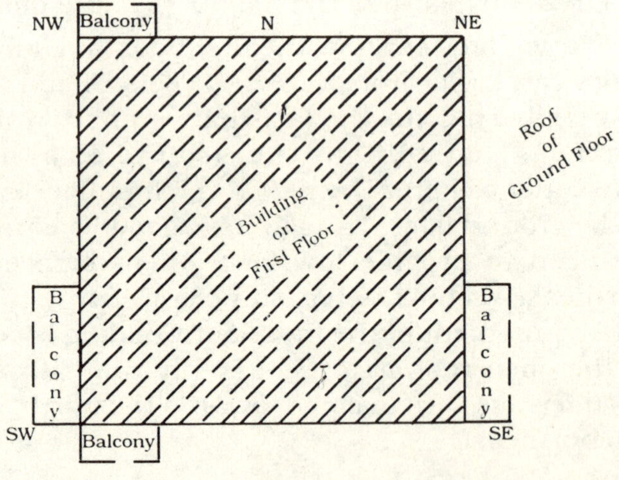

Fig 21

Fig (22) shows a structure with an extension in north, towards the northwest and empty space in the northeast. This results in a negative flow as firstly, the energy giving sector is missing and secondly the extension liberates negative field.

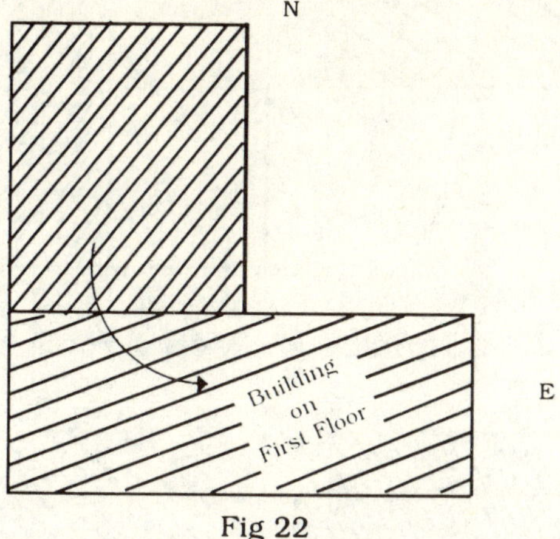

Fig 22

Extension of the building in the east-southeast (Fig 23), the south-southwest (Fig 24) and the west-southwest (Fig 25) again results in the same phenomenon as explained for Fig 22.

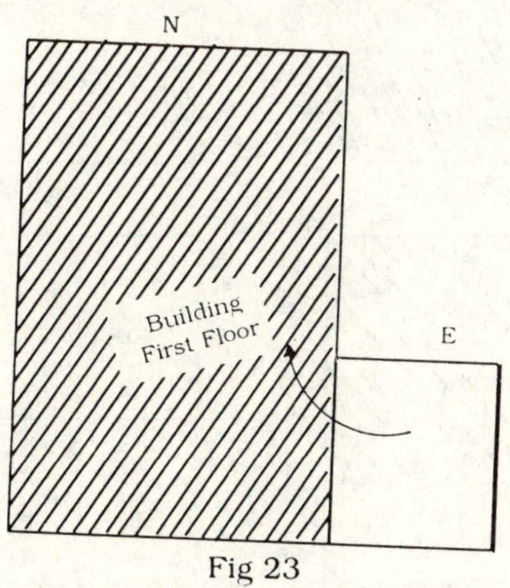

Fig 23

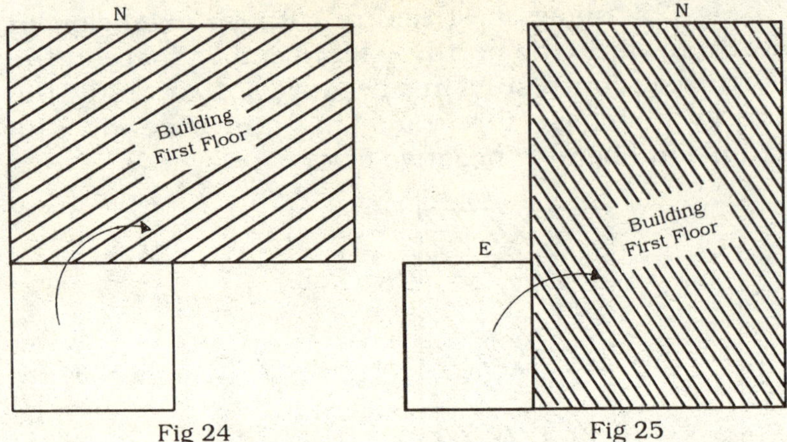

N
Building
First Floor

Fig 24

N
E
Building
First Floor

Fig 25

Fig 26, 27, 28 and 29 show open roofs in the wrong sectors.

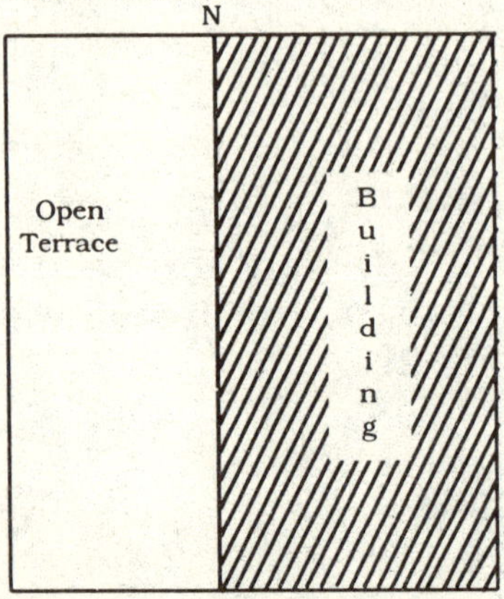

N
Open
Terrace
Building

Fig 26

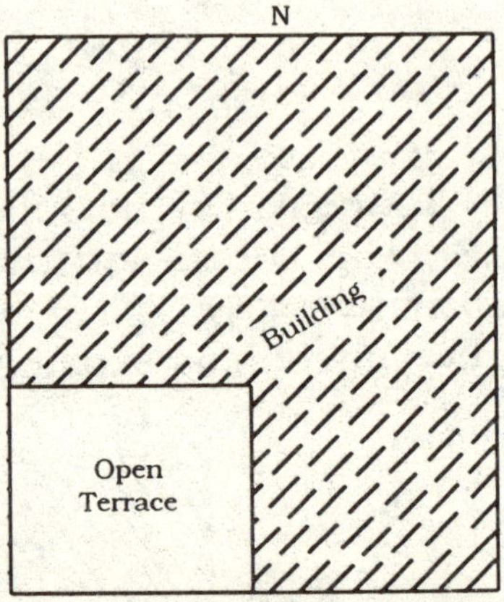

N
Building
Open
Terrace

Fig 27

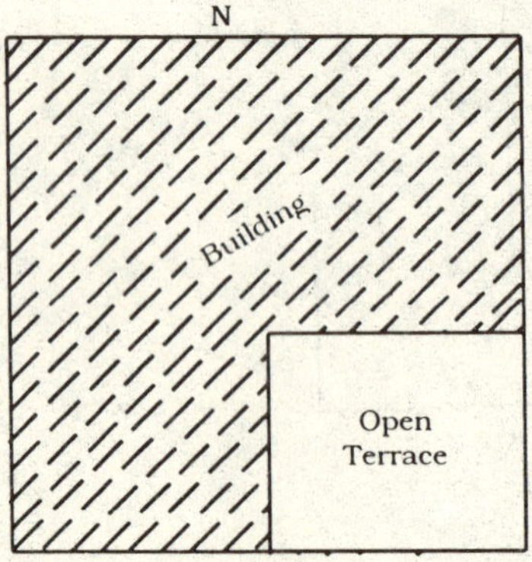

N
Building
Open
Terrace

Fig 28

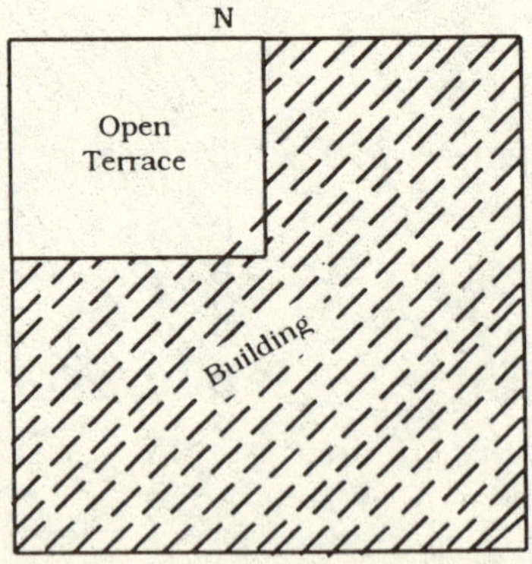

N
Open
Terrace
Building

Fig 29

As already stated open roofs are energy liberating. If they are open in the wrong sector, then the negative field becomes strong. In all these cases, the structure suffers from poor Vaastu.

A sloped roof which slopes from east to west

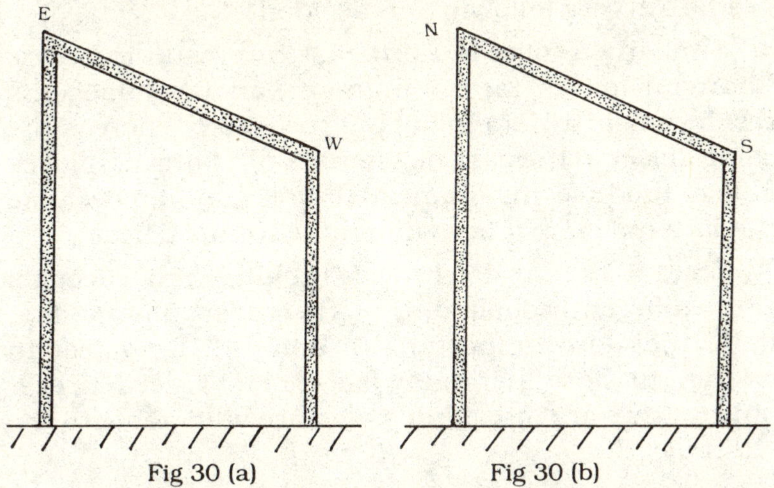

Fig 30 (a) Fig 30 (b)

Fig 30 (a) a north to south Fig 30 (b) or from north to south can effectively stop the flow of energy as higher levels in the roof weakens that particular sector. In a roof which slopes from east to west, the roof level is higher in the east than in the west. The southwest becomes more powerful in this case and the northeast is weakened which results in the structure turning negative. Same results follow if the roof is high in the north and low in the south.

We have now seen the defects that can occur in structures. We shall now see the effects of these defects. The effects vary depending on the purpose for which the building in question in used and the vulnerability of the individual concerned.

For example, a defective northeast in an industry can bring about production problems, whereas the same defect in a business house could lead to depressed sales. If this defect is present in a residence then it could cause health problems among the residents.

Again it is seen that a defect need not have the same effect on every family. For example, a kitchen in the northeast may aggravate the health problem of the eldest female in one house, but may act on the health of a male member in another house, while another may need a surgery following an accident.

Similarly a toilet in northeast can result in severe financial losses for a businessman who uses his residence partly for official purposes too. Whereas the same defect in the case of a houses of a bank employee fails to produce any financial distress on him because the latter is simply not vulnerable to this defect.

Thus a Vaastu defect in a building can affect its users differently depending on their own vulnerability. It is, therefore, important to analyse the defect in relation to the vulnerability factor and proceed further only if there are individuals who are vulnerable to the effects.

3

Problems faced in Structural Corrections

The ideal method of restoring a structure is by correcting the periphery and the structure which are defective to fall in line with Vaastu. There is obviously no equivalent to this approach. In almost all cases, the corrections if properly carried out, give desired results and the residents or users of the building can feel the change in the atmosphere almost immediately.

However, carrying out structural corrections through demolitions and renovations are often not practical or possible owing to the following factors:-

1. Building Byelaws

Every city has its own corporation which lays down rules for the construction of buildings. These are always not Vaastu favourable. For example, in Bangalore wider setbacks are allowed on the right side of the house for making driveways and for car garages. This means only a north-facing plot owner will have the good fortune of having higher setback in the east than in the west.

For a south-facing plot, the higher setback will be on the west side. As the minimum stipulated height is about ten feet for a 2400 square feet plot of size 60x40, the owner will have no alternative but to leave less setback on the eastern side. This automatically affects the peripheral energy field adversely.

Similarly in the case of an east-facing plot, the setback in the south will be more compared to the north. Although east-facing plots are preferred by people, but if they are to follow the byelaw, the Vaastu benefits will get affected.

Naturally all the houses, or at least a large majority of them have already adhered to these byelaws. In all these cases corrections are impossible as the byelaws are not sympathetic to Vaastu.

2. Strength of the structures

In case of existing buildings, another important factor is the feasibility of resorting to corrections keeping the age and strength of the structure in mind. Any concrete structure is supposed to last for a period of about 50 years. Thereafter it has to be raised to the ground and should be built afresh. In a developing country like ours, this is easier said than done. It is not surprising to see structures which are more than sixty or seventy years old where the residents are not even considering demolition but hope to continue there for their lifetime.

Even in cases where the inmates consider corrections as per Vaastu, it may not be possible to demolish walls and rebuild it as the strength of the structure would have been reduced considerably during the process of restoration due to aging. Restructuring old buildings by changing the position of the doors and windows is a formidable task as the 'lintel' technology was unknown in those times.

Again the "Madras" roof technology, which did not use reinforced concrete cement but relied on wooden girders with tiles to cast the roof, is another factor which makes structural corrections in many houses very difficult.

3. Practical Inconvenience

Many of the independent homes are built in accordance with the requirements of the owner. Whatever may be the Vaastu defects, it cannot be denied that the factors regarding convenience are well taken care of. Not all corrections can be carried out simultaneously ensuring the safety of the originally planned conveniences. Most of the people do not like to sacrifice the features which contribute to comfortable living in exchange for Vaastu benefits. All they want is the incorporation of Vaastu benefits along with the protection of the existing features. Because of the contradictory demands of the owner, carrying out structural corrections in the existing structure becomes impractical.

4. Apartments

In apartments the scope for structural correction is almost non-existent. Although you may be the owner of an apartment in a block you are not permitted to make any structural alterations as the walls, roof and floor are all shared among the various occupants. Short of disposing of the apartment you have no other choice here.

5. Rented Houses

Here again the problem remains the same as far as structural correction is concerned. Normally the owners are very reluctant to carry out corrections in their buildings as per the tenant's desire. Even when the tenant offers to pay for such corrections most of the landlords refuse as they fear that the looks of the building might get affected. They are also worried that the strength of the structure may be affected if extensive corrections are undertaken.

6. Reluctance

In any family it is too much to expect of everyone to think alike. If a few members of the family are in favour of any correction as they 'believe' in Vaastu the others more often oppose it. This is a normal situation in most of the households. In business enterprises the problem is more complex as the other partners may not believe in Vaastu at all, and hence, may show disinterest in carrying out structural corrections in the building. In all these cases, the effort of the few to get the building corrected structurally will be successfully foiled by others, resulting in a 'back to square one' situation.

7. Disruptions

In the case of an industry or a business enterprise, structural correction cannot be carried out without disrupting their daily regime. This means loss in terms of money. Depending on the extent of work involved it would be necessary to shut down the plant and give paid holidays to the workers for the entire duration of the renovation work. Most of the industrialists and businessmen are not understandably, receptive to such ideas.

Then there are some industries where the question of stopping the work itself does not arise as it may involve loss of several lakhs of rupees.

8. Layout Compulsions

In case of any industry or manufacturing unit the machines are so planned that the raw material fed at one end undergoes various operations and is delivered at the other end as finished goods. It will be unrealistic to expect the weight and the function of each machine to fall under the tenets of Vaastu and at the same time fulfilling the requirement of line manufacture. Thus a heavy machine involved in an intermediate operation may be installed in the southeast or northwest portions whereas a light machine may have to be placed in the southwest because of the requirements of the process involved.

Again in case of some industries, the process requires pit formation right underneath the machine.

Such machines are common in leather and silk reeling industries as a result of which the levels get disturbed. Similarly requirements of cold water, hot water and steam at various points may go against the Vaastu rules. While all these factors do contribute to the malfunctioning of the unit, there is obviously no possibility of correction by the conventional method.

9. Large plots

In case of large plots running into several acres, the correction of the levels cannot be carried out because of the costs involved. One cannot deny the fact that the amount spent on Vaastu corrections are rather hidden expenses and that there is no tangible result to justify the spending. If the same amount is invested in purchasing a gadget or in adding a block, the result of the expenditure is there for all to see. But in case of Vaastu correction, except the factor of bringing about mental satisfaction for the believer, there is nothing perceptible.

In case of large plots, factors like a hostile terrain rocks and mountains, canals and rivulets, etc. can all hinder in carrying out structural corrections even if one is mentally prepared to do so.

10. Roof Corrections

By far the most complicated part to be corrected is the roof. It virtually means that all the members occupying the building have to vacate the premises before this particular correction is resorted to. Dismantiling the roof is expensive and time consuming. Apart from this, one has to find a suitable alternative accommodation and shift all activities and household to the new premises before undertaking roof correction. Certainly not possible for a large family. All these broader problems and certain personal problems which vary from person to person makes one explore the possibility of Vaastu correction without demolition.

Certainly a need exists to explore this path and popularise it as well so that those who come under the various categories discussed above and are unable to take the conventional correction methods can have an alternative aid.

We shall discuss about these in the following chapters.

4

Corrections of Vaastu Defects through Feng Shui

Feng Shui

Feng Shui is a Chinese word which means wind and water. The concept of Feng Shui is not very different from Vaastu. The principle behind both are the same. Chinese refer to Chi as the cosmic breath and recognise that there is a male (positive) force and a female(negative) force which they call 'Yin' and 'Yang'. Just as Vaastu recognises that the entire universe is made up of five basic elements, the Chinese also recognise the five elements.

However the concept here is slightly different. In Vaastu, the five elements are earth, water, air, fire and ether (akasha) In Feng Shui the five elements are designated as earth, water, fire, wood and gold. Both sciences believe that the building should be oriented towards the north-south direction.

But there are irreconcilable differences as well. Feng Shui considers north as evil whereas according to Vaastu, the north is an auspicious direction, the ruling lord of the direction being Kubera, the lord of wealth.

Again Feng Shui declares that flow of water in the form of a canal or river or a rivulet in front of the building is auspicious, but Vaastu allows such flow only in the northeast direction and strictly forbids water flow in any other direction.

Feng Shui is also not without supersition. It takes into consideration the year of birth of the owner while choosing the plot.

Modern Interpretation of Feng Shui

Apart from these, modern Feng Shui practitioners lay a lot of stress on the surroundings. They try to 'read' what the surroundings actually mean. They believe that the appearances are an indication of the nature and the force present in that particular direction. For example, if a rock is found in front of the building then the Feng Shui practitioner carefully looks at the shape of the rock. If the shape appears to be of a huge giant with his mouth open then in all probability he would advise the owner to vacate the premises. According to him the rock signifies a force which wants to devour all the residents of the house and hence is not safe to live in.

The shape interpretation of surroundings is an important feature of Feng Shui. Feng Shui also pays importance to all the minor details. As per Feng Shui, there is no object which is too insignificant to cause trouble. Even a menacing looking door handle could be the cause of all problems inside. Similarly placement of furniture, directions that one should face and angles of the doors are all of primary importance in Feng Shui.

Unlike Vaastu, Feng Shui relies more upon the intuition of the practitioner. There are neither any rigid ground rules nor any inflexible application rules. After checking the building the Feng Shui expert arrives at some conclusions and then decides the 'cure'. The 'cure' could be a windchime, or a fishtank or a mirror or a rearrangement of the furniture. It could also mean a reorientation of your door or window.

Basically a Feng Shui cure ıs intended to block the negative forces from entering the building.

In this chapter we shall how fengshui cures can be employed to stimulate the environment inside a structure.

I may mention here that Feng Shui cures can be employed in two ways. One way is to apply them from individual point of view. Here if a person is looking for improvement in business then the cures are employed in the business premises. If he is an executive in a large organization looking for career advancement. Then the cures are employed in his office room. If he is looking for improvement in martial relationship then they are installed in the bedroom and so on. In the other words here the individual and what he desires most at that particular phase of his life are the guiding factors while placing the cures.

Feng Shui cures can also be employed for energizing various sectors of a house or apartment without bringing the individual in the picture. This procedure is ideal for homes and apartments where a family lives and the progress of all family members is desired.

The gadgets stimulate the environment in individual houses or apartments. If your house or apartment is against Vaastu then is worthwhile trying the Feng Shui cures.

Fire have a plan of your house or apartment. Look at the general shape of the plan. If it is a rectangle or a square then you can proceed further to install the cures.

If a corner is missing then a correction is called for. To find the missing corner divide the plan to nine equal parts as shown below.

North West	North	North East
West	Centre	East
South West	South	South East

Fig 31

Placing the plan in this nine square matrix you can determine which area of your house or apartment comes under the influence of a particular sector.

Ideally no corner should be missing in a house or apartment. But some times it is the case with houses and more so in case of an apartment. There is however no need to lose heart. All you have to do is to locate the missing corner. The defect can be overcome by using mirrors.

Let us take an example. In the following example you find that the northeast corner is missing. To re-establish the corner install two full-length mirrors at the places shown below. As you can see this gives an illusion of a northeast which is present.

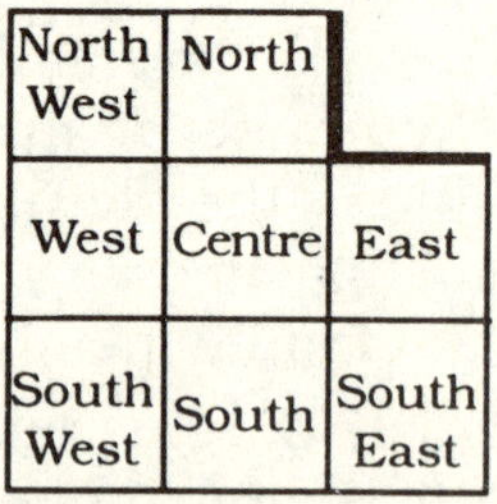

North West	North	
West	Centre	East
South West	South	South East

Fig 32

Any missing corner defect can be rectified by this method. However make sure that the mirrors are installed properly. Firstly a mirror used for this purpose should be of high quality without any distortions. Secondly you need a mirror which is of shoulder width and at least six feet in length. Two such mirrors are required.

The mirror should be permanently fixed on the walls. In the above case one mirror should be placed on the north wall and another on the east. The bottom line of the mirror should rest on the floor. Always use a single length. In other words you should not use more than one mirror to make up for the length.

In the rare case when you have more than one corner missing the same procedure is to be followed for the other missing corner also.

There is yet another possibility. You can have a building where a central direction sector is fully or partly missing. See the following figure.

North West	North	
West	Centre	East
South West	South	South East

Fig 33

You find that the North sector is missing in the building. In this case install a mirror of the same description as above at the point shown. This in effect restores the cut portion.

Once you have made sure that all sectors and corners are present, you can proceed to install the gadgets.

Feng Shui kits consist of various items. Let us learn more about them what are they—and what benefits they can give.

1. Pakua Mirror

A Pakua mirror is used to ward off wrong vibrations entering a building mostly through the main door. The wrong or harmful Chi will be emanating from a distant point due to secret arrows. It may be an ugly looking tree in front of your house or the roof line of the opposite building or the cross of a church or a temple tower. It may not always be possible to locate their origin. Secret arrows can get formed at great distances and the house can still be receiving bad Chi although you may not find any source of secret arrows in front or at the back of your building. It is therefore always safe to install a pakua mirror on the front door. If you have a back door to the house then it is advisable to have one more Pakua mirror installed over it so that both doors are safe.

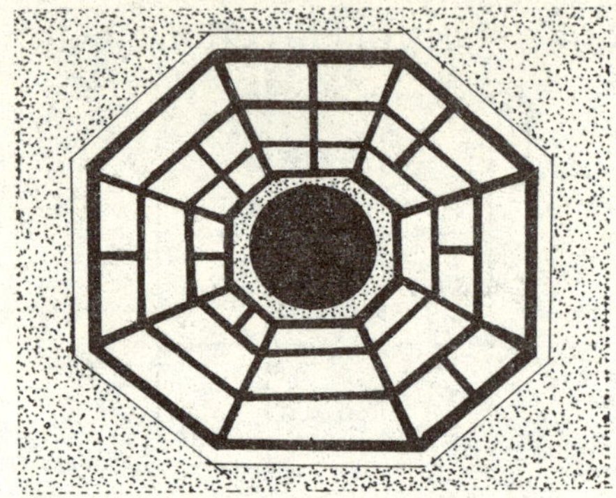

Fig 34— Pakua Mirror

A Pakua mirror consists of a round convex mirror mounted at the center of an octagonal shaped pakua. In the Pakua all sectors are represented with their respective colors and symbols. The octagonal plate is made out of high grade plastic to withstand out door use.

A Pakua mirror is to be installed outside only. It should never be used inside a building. Locate a place which is above the center point of the main door frame (or back door as the case may be) and roof line. Ideally it should be placed at equidistance from the roof line and door frame.

Hang the Pakua mirror with the help of the back hook provided after inserting a nail to the wall.

Hang the Pakua mirror with the help of the back hood provided after inserting a nail to the wall.

Mandarin Doves

The doves are made out of high quality wood and conform to the stipulated guide lines of Feng Shui masters. The pair consists of male and female. They should always be kept together one by the side of the other not one facing the other.

Fig 35—Mandarin doves

The ideal place to keep the Mandarin doves is the Southwest master bedroom. The exact location is unimportant. What is more important is that it should be placed at such a place then you can look at it while lying on the bed. They should be easily seen while entering the room or while leaving it. This cure is intended to improve the relationship between husband and wife and make life more harmonious.

They are also recommended to be placed in the room of a single woman or bachelor on the look out for a suitable life partner. It is believed by Feng Shui experts that marriage does take place in a short span if the doves are placed in the room of the needy.

Natural quartz crystals are energy enhancers. The crystal which is cut at different angles to reflect light all round energizes an area.

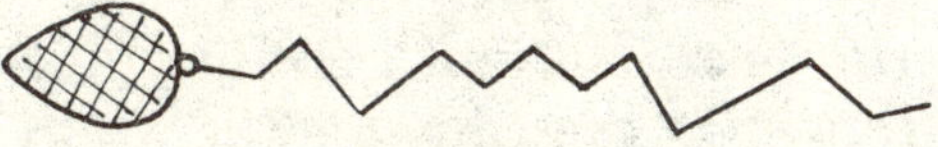

Fig 36

Ideally it should be hung in the Northwest corner of the building or in the Northwest room. It helps to improve relationships between the family members. It also brings in helpful people to your life. It improves money matters and brings good luck.

Prosperity Statue

Chinese attach lot of importance to symbols and figures. They believe every object is potent and vibrations emanate from it. Depending upon what the object stands for the vibrations may be good or bad. Thus objects which stand for violence like swords, guns, cannons always release negative vibrations and are best avoided in the interiors.

Feng Shui attaches great importance to statues that release helpful vibrations. One such very popular cure which is extensively used in Feng Shui is the prosperity statue. The statue is that of a happy, smiling, well-fed man carrying a bag of riches. (Fig 37).

Fig 37—Prosperity statue

The statue is to be kept behind you in the office above head level so that any visitor who calls on you for business purposes can look at it.

The statue is believed to release positive vibrations which go a long way in making the mind of the customer more receptive to your proposals.

In the house it should be so placed that when you open the main door you should be able to see it. Find a place or a showcase opposite the main door where the statue can occupy a prominent place.

Wind Chimes

Wind chime is one of the most frequently employed powerful cures. It is made out of very high quality brass tubes and powder coated to give lasting life free from corrosion. It is hand crafted to great precision so that the chiming goes on even when very little breeze is present. See fig 38.

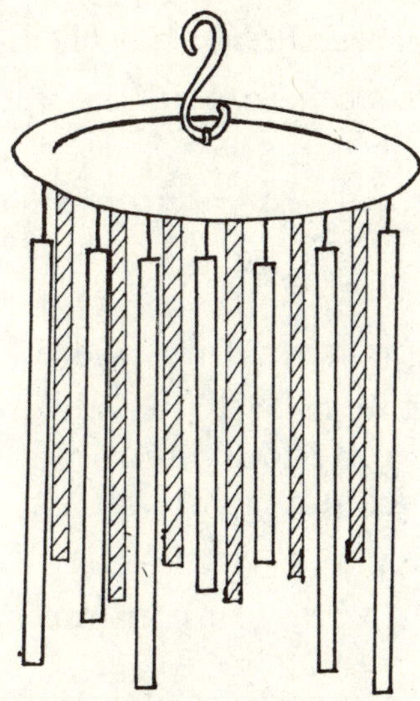

Fig 38—Wind chime

While installing the wind chime look for a place in your house or apartment where natural breeze enters all the time from a window. Again it will be best if the wind chime is installed as near the center of the house as possible so that the chiming sound is heard in every corner of the house. This is one way to make sure that the vibrations are indeed reaching and filling the entire building.

A wind chime is believed to neutralize the negative energy and stimulate good Chi. Surprisingly the belief of Hindus in this matter is identical to that of Chinese. Normally in every Hindu temple bells are installed and frequently sounded as you are well aware. All Hindu homes also have small pooja rooms in their dwellings where the bell is an integral part.

While performing any pooja the bell is sounded with the following mantra.

'Ghanta Nadam Kritva' (I am going to sound the bell so that—)

'Agamartantu Devaanam' (Divine forces enter—)

'Gamanartantu Rakshasam' (Devilish forces leave—)

'Kuru Ghantaravam Tatava' (By doing the sounding of the bell—)

'Devata Ahwana Lanchanam' (I am inviting the Gods)

Thus the use of the bell is associated from the olden days to create a positive atmosphere.

The advantage of a wind chime is that it is operational all twenty four hours and can ensure an atmosphere free from negative forces.

Celestial Animals

There are four celestial animals, one for each direction.

Animal	Color	Ruling Direction
Dragon	Green	East
Tiger	White	West
Phoenix	Red	South
Turtle	Black	North

The vibrations from any or all directions can be weak due to defects present in that direction or directions. Feng Shui holds that the directional attributes of every celestial animal can be restored inside the building by hanging the figures of celestial animals.

The celestial animal replicas are made in the stipulated colors on wooden plates. The plates are provided with a self adhesive sticker for easy fixing.

Fig 39

Ideally they are installed in the drawing hall where all family members assemble and where most of the time is spent together. Mark the center line of each wall with the help of a measuring tape. On the center line select a point which is about 7 feet from the ground. Repeat the procedure on other walls.

Now peel off the protective paper on the adhesive and stick the wooden plate at the point marked. Please note that the Dragon should be mounted on the East wall, the Tiger on the West, Red Phoenix on South and Turtle on the North wall. Leave it in place.

Once you have installed make sure that the dragon and the tiger are in one line. While sticking the figure ensure that the dragon's tail is towards north and so is the case with the tiger.

Door Pakua (Small)

Door pakuas are of two types. One is smaller than the other. A Pakua is similar in all respects to the Pakua mirror, the only difference being that in the center there is no mirror but the mirror is replaced with a YIN-YANG symbol.

The door Pakua comes with a red thread for easy hanging. The small Pakua is to be hung on the door frame of the master bed room. If you are using it in an office then it should be hung on the door frame of your office cabin.

A Pakua is believed to prevent wrong vibrations entering the room and also prevents the good vibrations leaving the room.

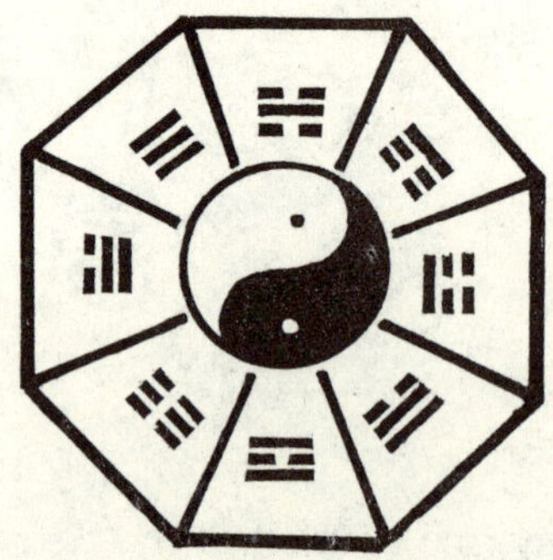

Fig 40—Main Door Pakua

This is of a bigger size compared to the room Pakua. It should be hung on the door frame of the main door. You need not put it exactly at the center if this comes in the way of entry. It can be suitably moved to a side.

Small Pyramid

Although pyramids are not a part of Feng Shui, it is a well known fact that they are liberators of positive energy. As we all know energy can neither be created nor destroyed. Kept in any negative atmosphere a pyramid converts the negative vibrations to positive ones and hence are a very helpful cure.

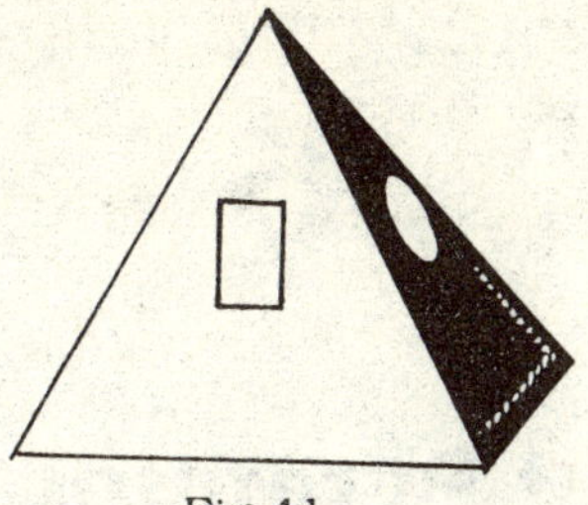

Fig 41

The small pyramid supplied with the kit is meant to be kept in a cash box to enhance luck in money matters. Busy executives who use their cars for business purposes will do well to keep a small pyramid in the glove compartment of the vehicle.

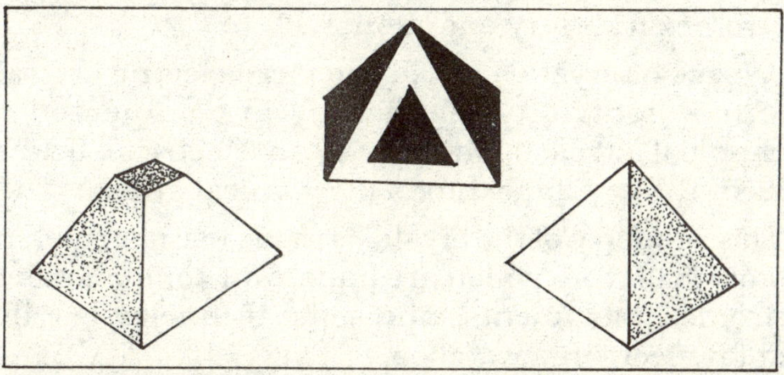

Fig 42

This is similar to the small pyramid in construction. It is to be kept on the northeast-southwest line to ensure unhindered flow of energy from northeast to southwest.

Keep the pyramid on a stool or cupboard after aligning it with the help of the compass supplied with the kit. The alignment should be such that the face marked North should face North direction.

Use of all the items as explained above can stimulate the entire energy field inside a building and help overcome the ill-effects of poor Vaastu.

5

Crystal Pyramids to the Rescue

Crystals which are found in Nature have certain unique properties which have helped in the growth of the Electronics industry enormously.

A class of crystals called the piezo electric crystals produce electricity when they are subjected to mechanical stress. Similarly if an electrical field is applied, the crystal exhibits mechanical stress.

This property of the crystal is made use of in making crystal oscillators which are important components in electronic instruments. The same technology is also used for electronic watches.

Crystals, according to clairvoyants, are closely connected with the cosmic intelligence and act as a mirror to what lies in store. Therefore crystal gazing is a favorite pastime of soothsayers. They gaze at a crystal ball to tell a person what lies in store for him in future.

You may also have seen the weekly forecasts which regularly appear in the popular dailies, some of which are derived through crystal gazing. They claim that they can see the future by just gazing at a crystal.

Recently I had the opportunity of meeting a European who was an expert on crystal power. He had a crystal which was cut at the top at various angles to improve its reflective powers and to improve the reflected energy. He placed the crystal as shown in Fig 43. It shows the plan and front elevation of the crystal.

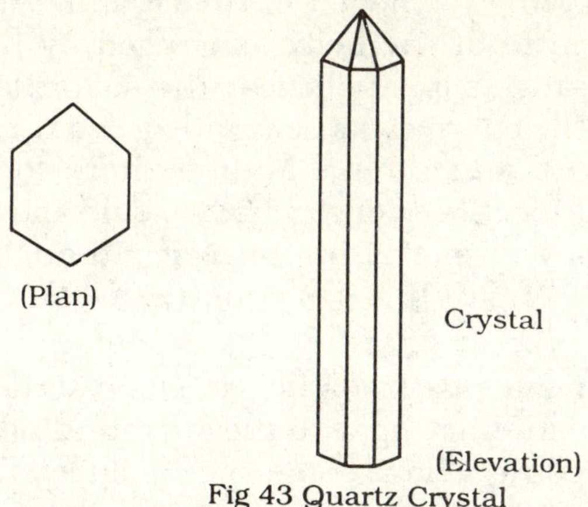

Fig 43 Quartz Crystal

Fig 44 shows how the crystal was arranged.

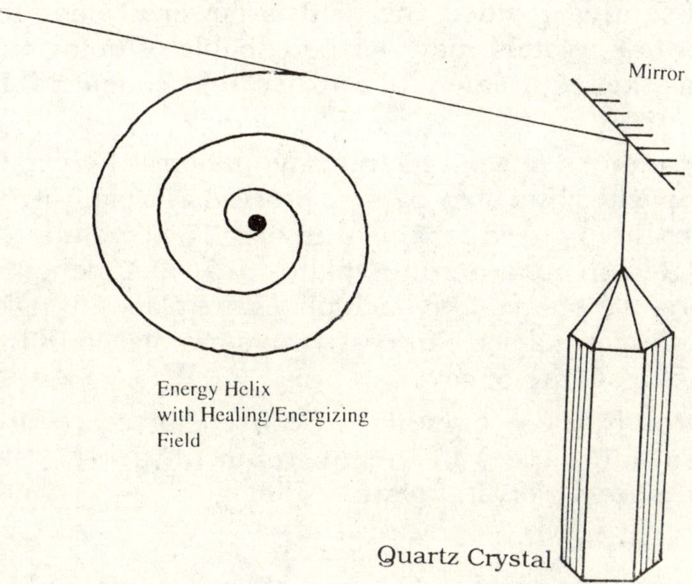

Fig 44

The crystal was kept upright on its base and placed on a table. A mirror was placed in line with the face of crystal at a distance of 2 feet. I was asked to move to the center of the helix. The gentleman informed me that the reflected rays from the mirror from all the six faces culminate to form an energy helix and that the helix would be lying to the left of the crystal. When I stood at the centre of the helix as gauged by him, I could feel a strange sensation near the solar plexus. He stated that the energy was being absorbed through the solar plexus and after standing there for five minutes I would feel very energetic. He said that this was a quick way of energising oneself although the healing effect of such a treatment is yet to be established.

What we can surmise from this is that crystals have a special way of interacting with the surrounding field and the reflected rays have some special effects.

It is reasonable to suppose that this field which is generated from the crystal can alter the Vaastu field significantly provided the field is powerful enough. Individual crystals may not be capable of doing the task as the requirement of a structure is considerably large.

By using a special technology millions of crystals are deposited by a step-by-step process. Normally ruby or sapphire is used for this purpose. The crystals are deposited on an aluminium plate of size 2x4 inches in a triangular shape. Two such plates are placed at right angles to form a set. Four such sets are placed in the form of a square to cover an area.

Initially these crystals were used for correcting natural imbalances in the environment. See Fig. 46 which shows a crystal plate.

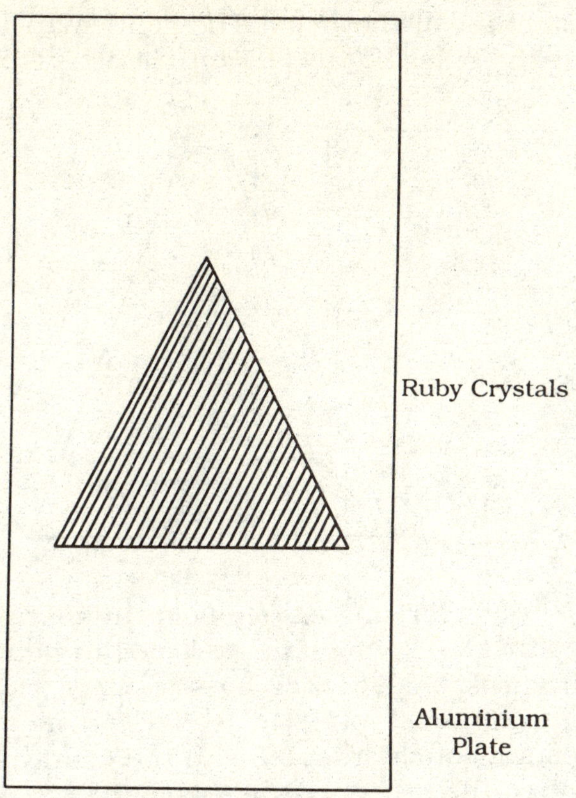

Fig 46 Crystal Plate

Fig 47 shows the configuration of the plates as mounted. The plates are always placed in a square configuration. The structure can be a room or a house or an industry or an agricultural plot.

Fig 47

It is surmised that the plate combination works by forming a polarising energy field as shown in Fig 45.

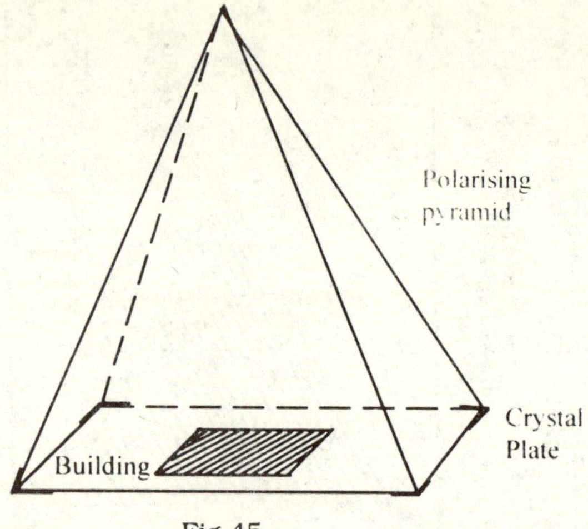

Fig 45

The polarising energy field thus formed produces negative ions which are believed to neutralise the ill effects of positive ions. One advantage with this system is that no electricity is needed as the crystals spontaneously interact with the energy field outside. The earth's own energy is therefore utilised to establish the polarising field.

A guaranteed effect of placing the plates in this manner is the elimination of all pests and insects from the building in the course of 3 to 10 days. These are a boon to a tropical country like India where every household has to wage a relentless and never-ending battle against insects. We no doubt use various chemical sprays to control them but these are hazardous for humans too. Inhalation of these vapours can produce harmful effects in the body.

The insects on which the plate energy is effective are ants, cockroaches, mosquitoes, aphids, termites, weevils, scorpions, ticks, white flies, grain moths, fruit flies, beetles etc.

The plates have proved their efficiency abroad in thousands of installations and are now available in India.

The installation of these plates are beneficial for elimination of all Vaastu defects where structural rectification cannot be carried out for one reason or the other. How do the crystal plates help in Vaastu rectification? Let us hypothesize.

We know that Vaastu is basically creating a harmonious energy field inside a structure. This is achieved by incorporating appropriate energy release areas and entry points as we have discussed earlier. A building with defective Vaastu produces a distorted field which creates distortions in the life of residents or its users also. Theoretically therefore if another energy field which is independent and more powerful than the distorted field is superimposed on the structure inside the field then the superimposed plot will be the one that is acting inside the structure also.

We all know that a pyramid can produce only a positive field. There are no negative areas inside it. Only areas with higher density and relatively lower energy density have been acknowledged so far. No areas inside the pyramid are known to cause harm to humans. Thus if the entire structure can be encompassed within a pyramid field, it should be able to counteract the ill effects of the distorted Vaastu field and create harmony once again.

Another area of application of these plates is in agriculture. As large areas are involved in farming, level corrections as per Vaastu are neither possible nor practical. One problem in an agricultural field with poor Vaastu could be poor returns in relation to the effort put in. Here again mostly the crops are lost due to pests which cause various diseases. The strain of the organism, causing the disease, changes frequently baffling the agricultural scientists time and again. The identification of a suitable antidote to counter the organism can be found only through a time-consuming study. All this is natural and understandable.

All the same, for the poor farmer, the losses are heavy. Recently we had this tragedy in Bidar where the crops were severely affected resulting in the ruination of several agriculturalists. Hence use of these plates, which are specially made to cover large agricultural plots, could be a God sent gift.

I am often questioned by skeptics— if it is harmful to pests, then wouldn't it be harmful for us as well?

Inside a pyramid matter does not putrefy. That means the growth of bacteria is discouraged inside the pyramid. The question arises as to whether an atmosphere which is harmful to an organism can be helpful to humans?

The answer is Yes. A colony of bacteria causes disease in humans. If such colony continues to flourish it would eventually bring the death of the host. We cannot deny the fact that, as the bacteria is flourishing inside the host's body multiplying every hour, the host is becoming sicker. Hence the relationship that exists between the host and the bacteria is not reciprocal. On the other hand use of antibiotics kills the bacteria, thereby helping the host. So obviously what is good for the bacteria is not good for the host and vice versa.

In Nature both destructive and constructive forces are at play. Any activity which involves growth must be positive and sustainable. If the growth itself becomes the cause of complete elimination, one can only term such a growth as destructive growth. When bacteria multiply in the host organism they are neither doing good to themselves nor to the host. An unchecked growth of bacteria can only mean the death of the host along with the bacteria.

A positive growth is a growth for the well-being of an organism and does not have an associated destructive side to it. Hence the philosophy that the energy inside is harmful to a disease-causing organism, but beneficial towards the well-being of an organism, who is in need of its own betterment, is quite understandable and acceptable. Hence there is no reason to feel uneasy about these energy fields.

As they are not very expensive to install one can give it a try. It could be one of the easy methods of eliminating Vaastu defects.

Note : *Crystal pyramids are available with—*

Catamaran Enviro & Trading Pvt. Ltd.,
301, Raheja Arcade, Koramangala,
Bangalore - 560095

Tel : 91-80-5530050, 5537750
Fax : 91-80-5532570
Delhi Office : 91-11-3550943/526353
Email : catamaran.blr@spinx.sprintpg.ems.vsnl.net.in
or
Sathya999@yahoo.com

6

Ionisers and Colors in Vaastu Corrections

We have seen in the earlier chapter how a rich negative ion field can be created by using crystal plates.

You should now know something about ions and their effects on us. The atmosphere surrounding us contains electrically-charged particles which can be either positively charged or negatively charged. These are called positive ions and negative ions respectively. While positive ions are harmful to the health, negative ions are conducive for a sense of well-being. It has been established scientifically that negative ions have a soothing and relaxing effect on humans.

An increase in concentration of negative ions increases the sense of well-being, whereas increased concentration of positive ion brings in a sense of unease. Further the dust around us, of which some of us are sensitive is the main cause of pollution and it is positively charged. The interaction of positive ions and negative ions in such an area can neutralise the charge on the dust particles and can bring them down harmlessly in a structure. However these negative ions will have to be supplied artificially to achieve this task.

It has been found that a chemical called serotonin, a hormone which is found in the blood, causes most of the health problems when the concentration of this hormone increases beyond a safe level. The surprising observation was that while injecting the anti serotinin brought the expected relief, the same relief was obtained by exposing the subjects to a stream of negative ions. Another advantage of negative ion treatment is that there are no side-effects, unlike medication.

An atmosphere rich in negative ions increases the ability of the blood plasma to absorb carbon dioxide. The rich negative ion atmosphere also contributes to better assimilation of food resulting in better repair functions of the body and growth of organism.

It is also reported that the open wounds heal faster in a negative ion atmosphere and infection of the wounds is also controlled in such an atmosphere.

Experiments have been carried out abroad to study the effects of concentration and relaxation responses in different ion atmospheres. It was conclusively demonstrated that the negative ion concentration in a room increases the alpha rhythm in the brain lobes and synchronized wave forms are emitted from the different lobes.

Acute anxiety syndrome responds well to the negative ion atmosphere. In the experiments conducted it was established that higher negative-ion concentration reduces the tension considerably.

Efficiency is directly related to the sense of well-being. It is, therefore, not surprising that the subjects exposed to negative ions performed better and showed better dynamometer response in the studies carried out.

It is interesting to observe that in an air-conditioned room, the natural flow of energy is obstructed which results in headache and nausea. Places, where computers are at work, the positive ion concentration is high and here again negative ion generators help to eliminate the problem.

Air-borne harmful bacteria are killed by exposure to negative-ion steams. This helps in the control of infections and the spread of infectious diseases.

It can therefore be safely concluded that negative ion generators have a role to play in creating a good atmosphere.

The following figure gives you the illustration of an ioniser.

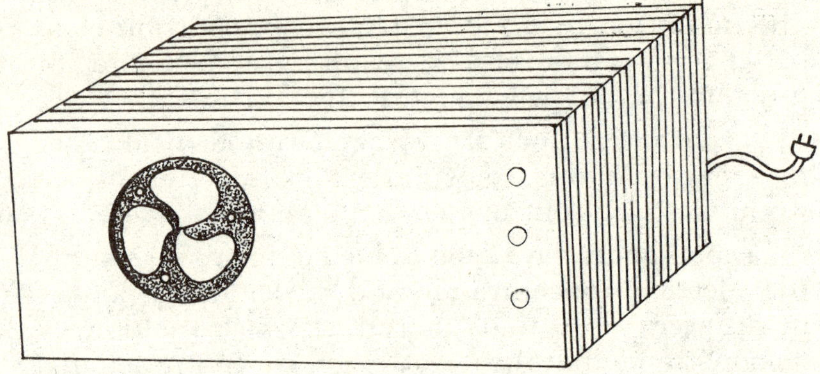

Fig 48—An Ioniser

Colors as Compensators

Colors have profound effects on both the body and the mind. This face was recognized centuries back by the ancient Indians. In one of the ancient texts called the *Kurma Purana* the importance of the colours has been beautifully illustrated.

The author has carried out certain experiments in cases of apartments and buildings where conventional corrections were not possible. It has been found that a wrong energy flow in a sector can be balanced to a great extent using complementary colors. Let me cite an example here. Normally, a bedroom is not provided in southeast. When such a bedroom is used by a teenager or an adult, they tend to become irritable and short-tempered. Most of the people who sleep in such bedrooms complain of disturbed sleep and nightmarish dreams. It is seen that the effect gets compounded if the room has a blue coloured wall. However, if the room has an off-white or pink coloured wall, the effect comes down considerably. By using yellow colour on the walls, it is seen that the ill-effect of the southeast completely disappears and the room becomes cheerful. It can function as a satisfactory study room or bedroom for any member of the family.

Rooms in the south are to be painted white without any colour to energise them. In case the kitchen is moved to south or if there are bathrooms or toilets in south, use white colour. Again here it is observed that green colour produces illness and blue colour makes the person dull.

Another possibility is not having a master bedroom in southwest. There are quite a number of houses where the kitchen is in southwest. In all such cases where the room in the southwest is used as a kitchen, paint the room with an orange colour and use orange-coloured glazed tiles to ward off the ill-effect of utilizing the area as a kitchen. It is seen that in most of the houses where the kitchen is in southwest, the health of the family members, especially the ladies, is adversely affected. By using orange colour both for the walls and the tiles, the effect gets completely eliminated. Similarly, the kitchen platform should be made out of pink granite and not black granite, as is the case normally.

In case the master bedroom is in northwest corner, using blue colour stabilizes the energy field there. People who use northwest bedrooms have experienced thoughts crowding them at night. They are also seen to suffer from too many dreams disturbing their sleep. The ill-effect is because of the characteristics of northwest energy which is unsteady by nature. Northwest corner is basically meant for bath and toilet purposes. This problem can be completely eliminated by using blue colour. You will find that once the walls are painted blue and the curtains are changed to light blue colour, with a blue light serving as a bed-lamp, the atmosphere becomes cozy and the sleep pattern changes to a deeper, more restful one.

While using colours one should always remember that the shade of any particular colour used should be light. Never use dark, heavy colours in any place of the house. Secondly, the window and door curtains should have the same colour shade as that of the wall. These two factors are important to get the best benefits.

In case of west rooms, used for a wrong purpose like kitchen, drawing or fire, use pink colour to stimulate the area. The rooms in east should have light, cheery green colour on the walls, whereas rooms in the northeast should have ultramarine or offwhite colour on the walls. In case your house does not conform to Vaastu, then before considering shifting or selling go for colour change and see the effect.

In case you have projections in the rooms in the wrong corner, paint the room in the colour explained above and only the projected area should be coated with a bright, white colour. This eliminates the effect of a wrong projection. In most of the cases, colour correction is simple and inexpensive to adopt to. It should be tried wherever other methods cannot be implemented due to one reason or the other.

7

Pyramids for Correcting Residential Plots

What are Pyramids?

Most of you must have heard the word pyramid. It is a Greek word meaning 'Fire in the Center'. Hence we can understand that pyramid produces energy at the center or rather it is an energy generator.

According to the law of conservation of energy which is accepted by the scientific community, energy can neither be created nor destroyed. It can change from one form of energy to another. We see this all around us in our daily life. Electric energy gets converted into light energy to brighten our homes, gets converted into heat energy to heat the bathing water and gets converted to mechanical energy to drive the pumps etc.

Thus if the pyramid has to supply energy or if the energy has to get liberated at the center then this energy will have to be obviously supplied from the surrounding space. As mentioned earlier we live surrounded by various types of energy and it is this energy which enters the pyramid from the various sides and interacts inside to release another form of energy.

A pyramid is basically an object which has four triangular sloping sides with a flat base. See the following figure to understand the structure of a pyramid. The tip of the pyramid is pointed and is called the apex.

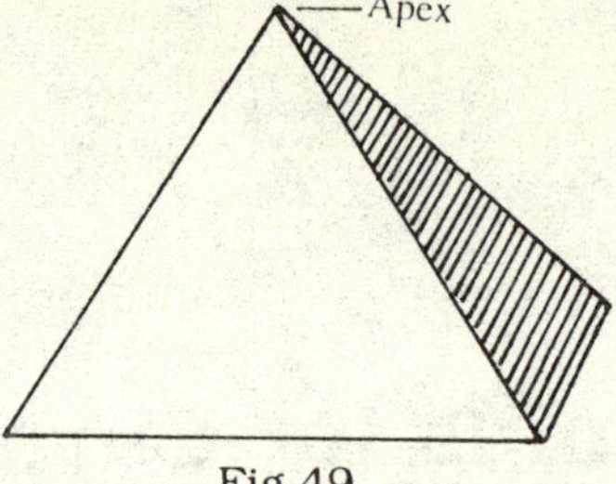

Fig 49

Pyramids abound in Egypt which is called the land of pyramids. The world's largest pyramid called the pyramid of Giza is found here. This pyramid is estimated to be about 450 feet high and is estimated to comprise two million stones. The granite blocks used here weigh somewhere between two to seventy tons. Even today it is a mystery as to who built it and when. Various theories have been proposed, but none have been accepted as final.

Experiments carried out on small pyramid models essentially conforming to the dimensions of the pyramid of Giza of have conclusively proved that, inside the pyramid a distinct atmosphere exists which is protective and energy giving. It also appears that the energy emitted from the apex and from the base are like the male and female parts of bioenergy and the energy which is released at around one-third the height from the base inside the pyramid is akin to bioenergy.

Experiments have also shown that the energy which gets released from the apex is hot in nature whereas energy released from the base is cold in nature. Probably the three types of energy released from the pyramid are comparable to the *vata*, *pitta* and *kapha* concepts of ayurveda and the pyramid is a device where all these three forces exist in harmony. Pyramids are being used for rejuvenation and healing all around the world.

Alignment of the Pyramid

The pyramid of Giza is so aligned that one of the sides faces exactly towards the north. Normally in experiments which are carried out to tap the energy, this alignment is made use of. It is also observed that irrespective of the alignment, a certain energy gets continuously released inside the pyramid. But if the alignment is disturbed, it does not mean that the energy inside completely disappears. It only means that it is not working at an optimum capacity.

When the pyramid is so aligned that the four sides face the four cardinal points, it is said to be in the axis. Yet another method of alignment tried out by me is cross aligning the pyramid where the four faces look at northeast, southwest, northwest and the southeast instead of the north, east, south and the west.

In Vaastu these directions are basically more important than north, south, east and west. All those who have studied this science are well aware that the defects in these directions produce far more serious effects than the defects in the east, north, south and west directions.

Taking a cue from here I conducted experiments by aligning the pyramid on its edges in a way that each edge faced towards each cardinal direction. See the following figures.

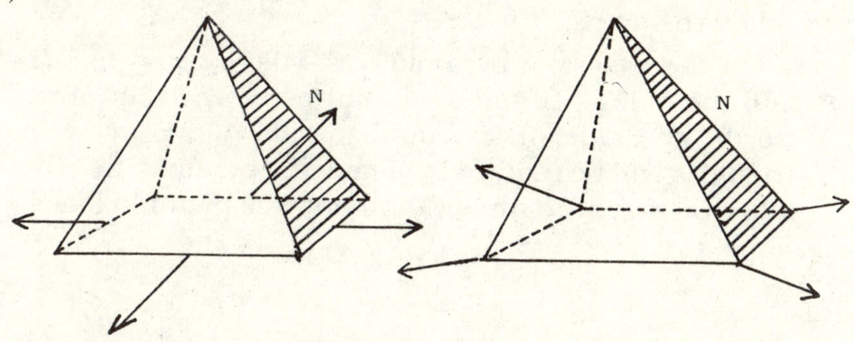

Fig 50—Standard Alignment

Fig 51—Cross Alignment

It is interesting to note that pyramids with eight faces called Astamoga pyramids appear to have energy which is several times the energy produced in a regular pyramid. In an astamoga pyramid, while four faces are aligned towards the north, east, south and the west, the other four faces are aligned towards the southwest, northeast, northwest and southeast respectively.

It appears that the extra energy which gets released in the astamoga pyramid is primarily due to the energy interaction from the four cross directions. A pyramid which is aligned on a cross axis functions much better as far as the effective elimination of Vaastu defects are concerned.

I would, however, like you to try both the straight and the cross alignment and then come to the conclusion as to which one works best in your plot. This is because it is difficult to determine which sector is defective in a plot. It could also be a case of the involvement of more than one sector. Thus if the defects of the north, east, west and south sectors are causing the problem then aligning it as per the standard practice could be better. If on the other hand the cross directions namely northwest, southwest, southeast and northeast are involved, then it is better to cross align the pyramids for Vaastu corrections.

In the figure given below BC is called as the base and AB and AC are called as the sides. The point A is called the apex.

In the case of a pyramid, BC will be equal to 9.5" and the sides AB and C should be 9" each. In other words, the side AB is equal to side AC. Four such triangles will be required to make the pyramid. See the following figure to understand how the pyramid looks.

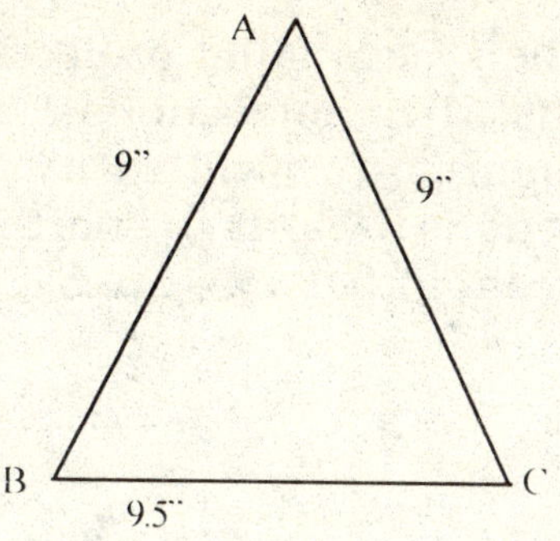

Fig 52

The pyramid has to be buried in the soil, hence wooden pyramids should not be used for the purpose. Moreover it is difficult to control the dimensions while dealing with such small sizes in wood.

Plastic pyramids are the best. These can be made from PVC and bakelite.

We shall now see how to correct the angular defects by using pyramids.

Angular defects arise due to the extension of a corner of a plot at a particular angle other than the northeast. Angular projection towards the northeast enhances the quality of the plot and should be retained for best benefits. In such a situation no correction is called for (Fig 52).

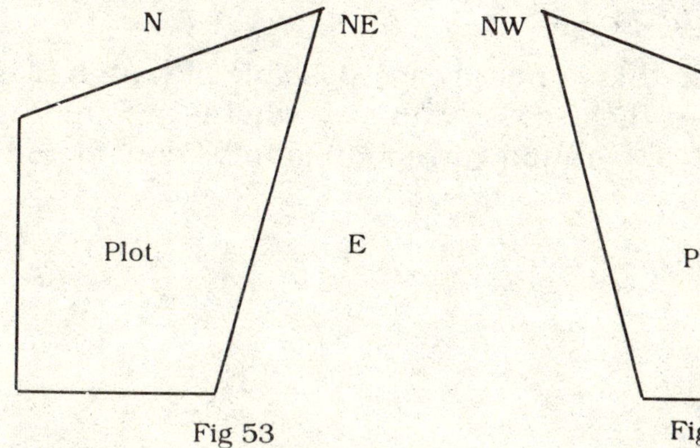

Fig 53
Projection of North East
No correction required.

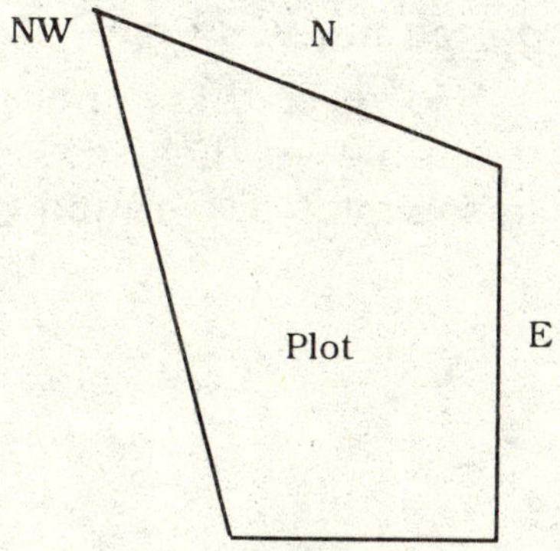

Fig 54
Projection of
Northwest

However when the angular projections are towards other directions, then corrections are called for. See the following figures. You will see that the plots have defective projections towards the northwest, southwest and the southeast in figs. 55, 56, 57.

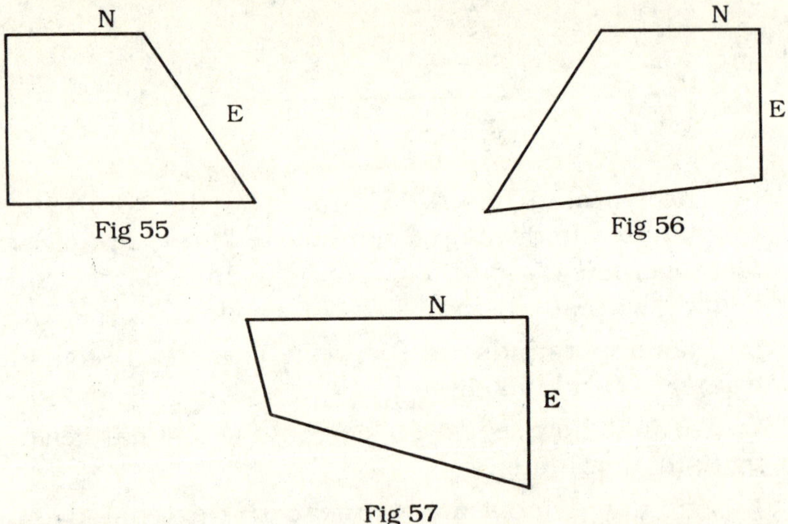

Fig 55

Fig 56

Fig 57

In these cases the normal procedure recommended for the correction of the plot is by building compound walls so as to carve out the maximum rectangle or square from the distorted plot. The areas that can be carved out if this procedure is adopted is shown in the dotted lines in Fig 58.

However this is not always possible although it is desirable. In these cases and also where the building has come up, pyramid correction is to be considered.

Installation

See the following figure.

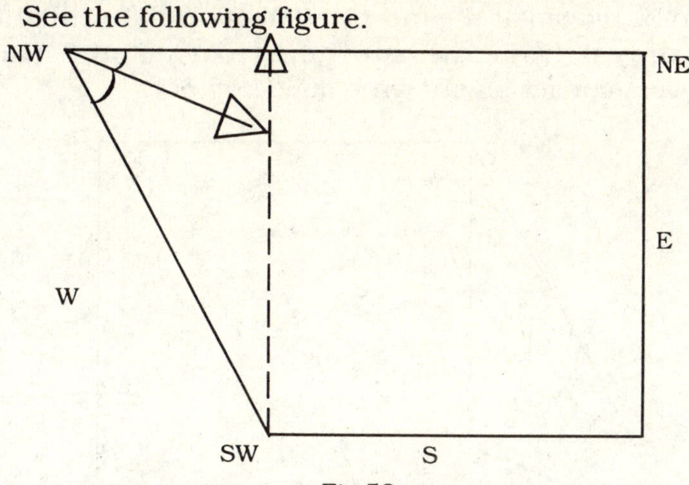

Fig 58

In the above plot there is Northwest projection.

To nullify the effect of a strong northwest, draw a line which would correct the plot to form a rectangle. Install a pyramid on the point where the line from the southwest meets the line from northeast. One more pyramid to be installed at the point where the bisector of the angular defect meets the imaginary line.

In a plot where the southeast is projecting, the pyramid should be placed at the intersection of the straight lines drawn from the northeast and the southwest as shown below. (Fig 59)

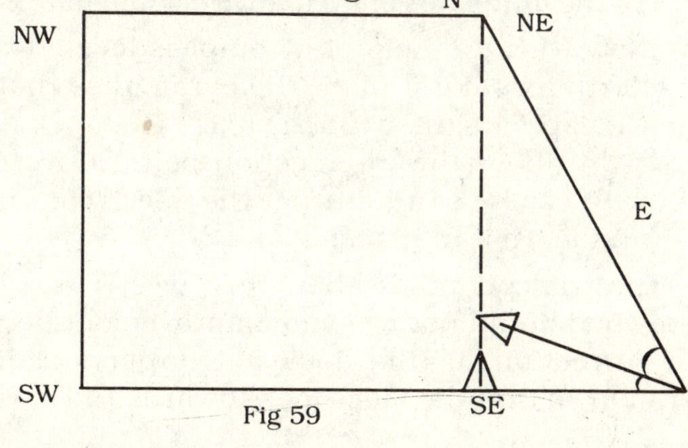

Fig 59

In a plot where southwest is projecting, the pyramid should be placed at the intersection of the two straight lines drawn from the southeast corner and the northwest corner as shown below. (Fig 60)

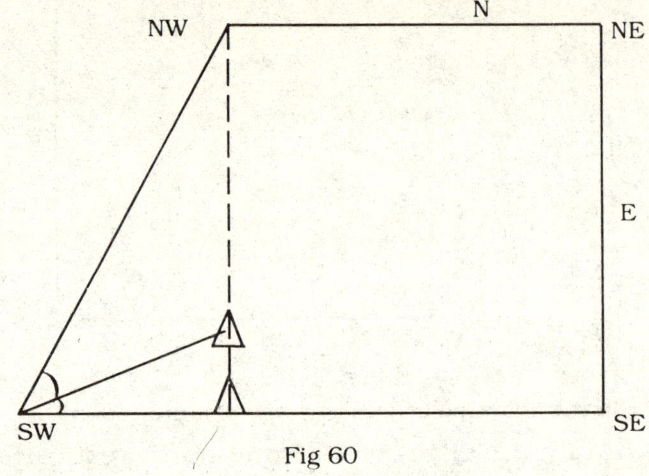

Fig 60

The installation of the pyramid is to be done as under:

(i) Dig a pit of about 30cmx30cm, with a depth of 20cm. The pit must be a square and the center of the square is the point where the two lines drawn, as explained above, intersect.

(ii) Place a white marble slab of a thickness of about 10mm at the bottom of the hole. Likewise cover all the four sides of the pit with white marble slabs.

(iii) Now with the help of a compass locate the exact north axis. First place the pyramid so that one of the faces aligns with the axis. The apex must be right above the intersection point. Cover the pit with coarse sand, but let the apex remain visible and leave it in place.

The trial period is about two weeks and by that time you should notice some improvement because of the correction. If this does not happen realign the pyramid so that the faces look towards the northwest-southeast. If the first alignment does not work, the possibility is the second alignment will work.

The pyramid combination to be installed in an irregular plot is discussed in the following chapter.

8

Pyramids for Correcting Agricultural/Industrial plots

For Large Areas running into several acres it is not possible to correct the corners because the contours may not fall into any known geometrical shape. Under such circumstances, it is better to go for a center point correction which will effectively negate the adverse implications of a distorted Vaastu field.

Apart from irregular contours the other area where pyramid combination is recommended is where the levels are not as per Vaastu.

However a pyramid correction should be considered only as a last alternative after exploring the possibility of other conventional correction methods.

This is because we are dealing with energy fields here which are subtle and there is no instrument to measure it conclusively. For countering an energy field you require another equal and opposite energy field. If we can measure one, we can design the other.

In other words a structure has, depending on its size, a definite energy-level requirement to sustain the residents inside but we cannot measure it. If there is a deficiency, then the residents have problems in matters of health and happiness.

No doubt a pyramid combination gives an additional supply, but how much? Is it enough to make up the shortfall? If not, the problem may continue to persist in spite of the pyramid combination.

The pyramid is basically a universal energy convertor. It is Nature's law that energy can neither be created nor can it be destroyed. However, every object in the universe is surrounded by various energy fields. All a pyramid does is to convert the surrounding energy fields to *pranic* energy field. The face of the pyramid does not pose any obstruction for the energy field to penetrate the inside of a pyramid. A properly aligned pyramid requires different types of energy from four directions, viz. north, south, east and west. The interaction of the energy thus received takes place inside the pyramid at $1/3^{rd}$ the height from the base.

The energy that is released from each pyramid is a strong type of bio-energy and can also eliminate distortions inside the structure. The idea of installing the pyramid combination at the centre is that the centre of a buiding is where all the forces converge and disperse. The old texts like *Mayamata* and Vishwakarma's *Vaastu Shastra* have given great importance to the effect of the center which is also called as the *Brahmasthan*. The old masters had stipulated that any type of load like a pillar or a staircase should never be present in the *Brahmasthan* and for all practical practical purposes it should be left free. In fact, this practice was scrupulously followed in the construction of the old buildings and even toady one can see such buildings in villages and small towns where the central portion was left open to the sky.

With the increase in population and the acute shortage of space, i.e. the *Brahmasthan* was also covered with the structure. The idea of putting the pyramid combination at the centre is to invigorate the central point so that the distorted energy inside the structure is neutralized.

Take nine pyramids of 235.5mm base length. The side length of this pyramid will be 236.6m and the centre height will be around 150mm.

Preliminary Stages of Correction

To carry out structural corrections, first the center of gravity of the plot has to be determined. In an regular plot, the process is easy, but in case of irregular plot, it becomes a long-drawn process. We will discuss the different steps to determine the center of gravity of your plot.

(a) Finding the center of gravity of a regular plot

If the shape of the plot is a rectangle or a square, irrespective of the size, you can locate the center of gravity by joining the diagonals. It is advisable to make an accurate drawing and first locate the center point on the drawing. Fix the coordinates of the center which can then be transferred to the actual plot and the exact center determined.

See the following example where I have shown how to determine the center of gravity of a square and rectangular plot.

Fig 61 shows a square plot. In a square plot, the length is equal to the breadth and all the four sides are equal. Let us say that the length of each side is A feet. Now by joining the diagonal, you will find that the two diagonals intersect. Let us call this point O. O is the *Brahmasthan* or the point of centre of gravity.

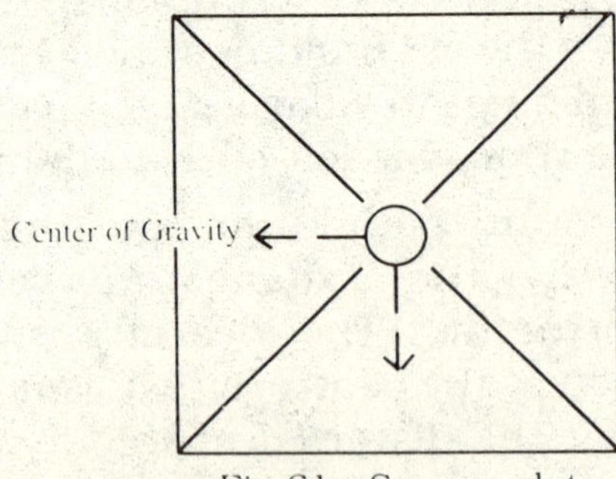

Fig 61—Square plot

See figure No. 62 Here the plot is a rectangle. In a rectangle the length and breadth of the plot will be different. Here B shows the length of the plot and A shows the breadth of the plot in feet. Again by joining the diagonals, the intersection point, which is the centre of gravity, can be found.

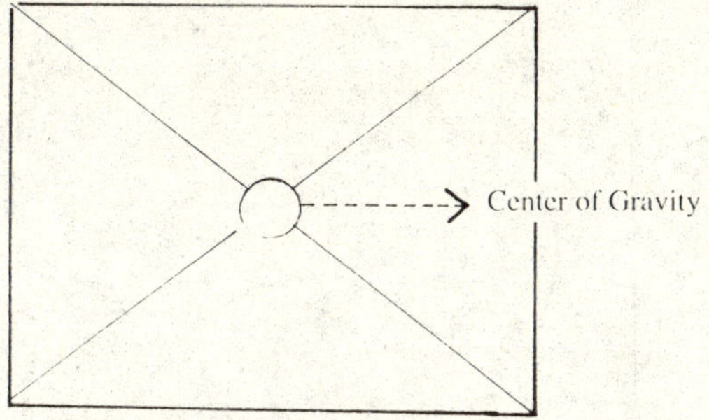

Fig 62—Rectangular plot

To actually transfer the center point to the plot you need three or four fixing dimensions. Select the dimensions as under. This is to only make sure that while transferring and fixing the point on the actual plot you do not err.

These points are to be used if you are unable to join the diagonals. Even if you are able to join the diagonals it is always better to double check the location of the center point by determining the point from an alternative dimension. After you fix the center point, drive a peg at that point so that the location can be easily located when needed.

(b) Finding the center of gravity of an irregular plot. In case of large plots, the shape of the plot may not fall into any mainly known geometrical shapes like a square or a rectangle. If the area is large but still shaped like that of a triangle or a rectangle, then you can easily determine the center of gravity by just joining the diagonals as explained earlier. However, if the shape of the plot is irregular, then the centre of gravity will have to be determined by a different method. Here are cases of some plots which are irregular in shape.

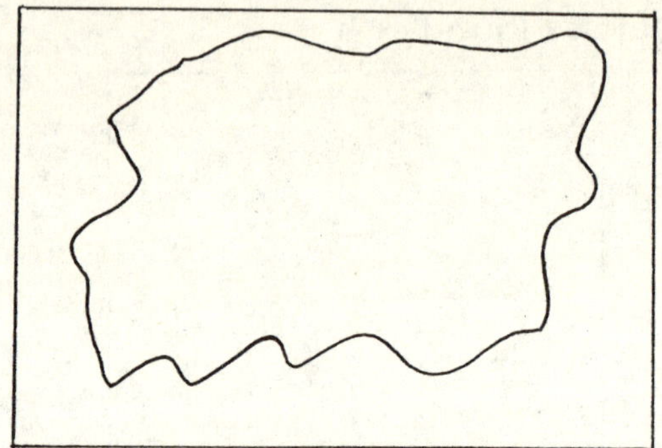

Fig 63—Contour map

In these cases, the total area under your ownership can extend to several hundred acres of land. In such cases, to determine the center of gravity of the plot, you will first of all need an accurate revenue survey map. This is normally provided by the revenue authorities, demarating the area which is under your ownership. Obtain a revenue survey map before you proceed further. Once the revenue survey map is obtained, there are two ways of finding the centre point. They are :

1. Through the cad/cam facility.
2. Cardboard.

1. Through the cad/cam facility : Any cad/cam service provider can help you if you give him the revenue survey drawing, with the help of the software they have, they will mark the exact centre of gravity of your plot and give it back to you. This type of service is provided by most of the computer companies having cad/cam machines.

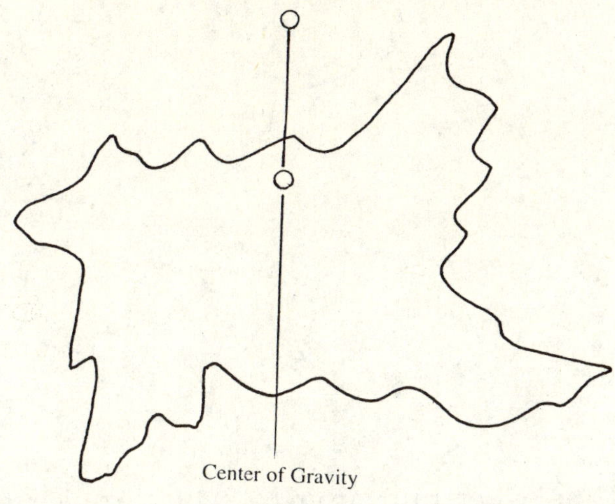

Fig 64(a)

2. Cardboard: In case you are unable to obtain the services of a cad/cam agency, you can adopt another method. Take a cardboard of about 6mm thickness and large enough to cover the full revenue survey map. Take an extra copy of the revenue survey map and using a pair of scissors carefully cut out the contour area. Paste that contour area on the 6mm cardboard and mark the contour properly. Using a pair of scissors cut out the contour on the cardboard. Now you have a miniature replica of the shape of the plot on your 6mm cardboard surface. With the help of this cardboard you can now determine the centre of gravity. Make 3 to 4 holes approximately 90^0 from each other near the edge of the cardboard. Hang the cardboard from each hole and draw a straight line to the other end of the cardboard. See the following figure to understand this spot more clearly.

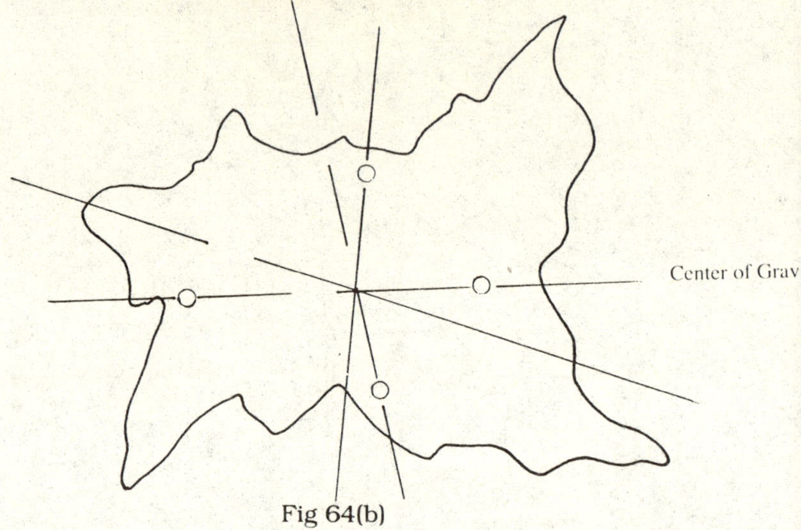

Fig 64(b)

Thus, when hung from each hole, you get a straight line, each line running across the board. You will find that from each hole you get a straight line which meets the other line at a particular point. This is the centre of gravity of the plot. Now, approximately measure from each point where the centre of gravity lies. For this purpose, you should use some known landmarks like a tree, well, bush etc., which are near the edge. After determining the length on the cardboard, transfer the dimension to the actual area.

Installation of the Pyramid Combination

A combination of nine pyramids has to be placed as under. Take nine pyramids of 235.5mm base length. The side length of this pyramid will be 236.6mm and centre height will be around 150mm. At the center, dig a pit 1.25mx1.25m. Place the pyramid in the center of each pit. After the pyramids are placed, the pit will look as under.

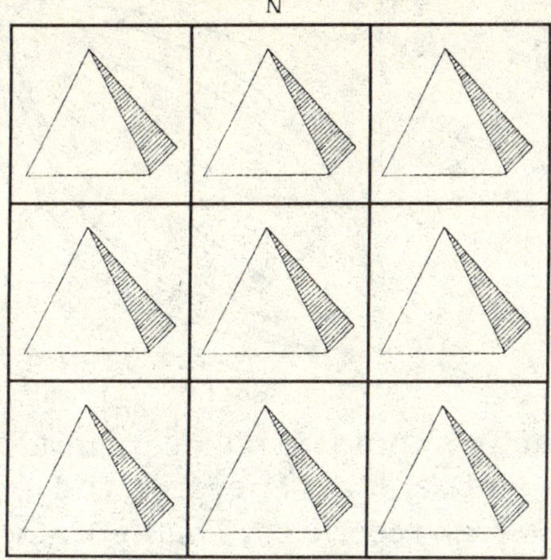

Fig 65

Take sufficient quantity of small pebbles similar to those used in fish tanks. Your local aquarium shop will supply this material to you. Fill the pit carefully using the pebbles without disturbing the position of the pyramids. Leave the tips of the pyramids uncovered.

Cover the pyramids with a flat asbestos sheet along the whole area.

If you are working on a large plot, it is better to cordon-off the area with a barricade and then do some landscaping so that vehicles do not pass over it. This will also save you the trouble of explaining to everyone what you are up to!

The method eliminates or at least suppresses the negative influences in the plot. Let us speculate how this pyramid combination works.

First of all we have to understand how a Vaastu defect interferes with the energy liberated in a plot.

See the following figure. You can see that a square and level plot compounded on all four sides establishes an energy flow from the northeast to southwest.

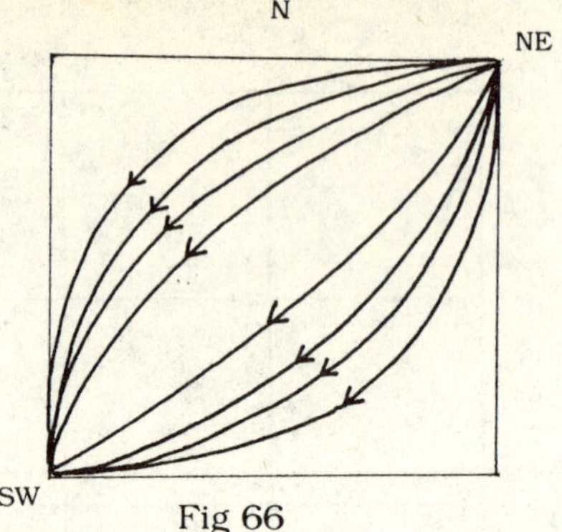

Fig 66

One factor should be borne in mind here. Note that it is the plot which generates the energy and the structure which receives it. Theoretically therefore three things can go wrong.

1. The plot generates the energy as it is specified by Vaastu but the structure is so oriented that it does not receive it.

2. The structure is as per Vaastu, but the plot does not generate enough energy as it does not follow the principles of Vaastu.

3.Both the plot and the structure do not follow the tenets of Vaastu.

In all these cases, a distorted field is present in the structure which eventually affects the health and happiness of the occupants or the users of the building.

We will now see how plot defects can cause distortion in the energy field.

See the following figure.

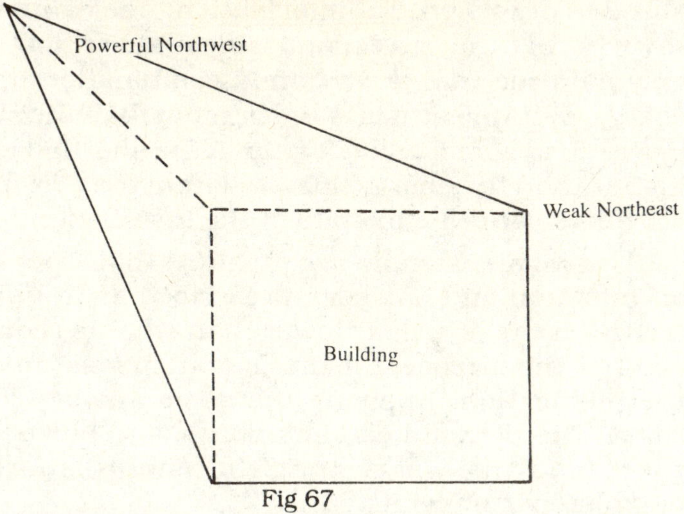

Fig 67

The figure shows the plot which has an acute angle projection in northwest. Because of this, angle at northeast opens up and becomes obtuse. An obtuse angle at any corner stands for a weak energy potential. Whereas, an acute angle at any corner stands for a powerful potential. The aim of Vaastu is to have an acute angle in northeast so that the northeast energy is very powerful and have obtuse angles in northwest and southeast so that the energy flows easily from northeast towards southwest.

In the above case, the northwest which has a negative potential becomes more powerful than northeast. Energy variation from northeast having been completely neutralized by the higher potential at northwest, the plot becomes useless from the point of view of Vaastu.

To compensate this we have to create an additional field inside the plot. This is done by using a combination of pyramids.

One factor must be borne in mind. There are no instruments to measure the energy liberated by a pyramid. Neither do we have any instruments to determine the exact shortfall in a structure. In the absence of this crucial information, one cannot really say whether the correction is adequate or not. We can only concede that the pyramid combination liberates energy. But unless it is equal or more than the shortfall in the structure it will not help. If the shortfall is much higher than the energy liberated from the pyramid, the ill effects continue in spite of the installation.

To give an example, we presume that a person has an infection and has been prescribed an antibiotic as a cure. If the dosage is lower than what is required to combat the disease, the disease will persist in spite of the medication. Applying the same analogy, we find that if the pyramid combination has to be successful then it is necessary that the energy shortfall is completely compensated.

If no relief is observed after the installation of the pyramid, you can conclude that the energy supplement is not adequate. One comforting factor is that the pyramid combination is not expensive to install. Hence even if it fails you will not have incurred a very heavy expenditure. When no alternative, other than undertaking expensive demolition or vacating the premises are the only choices left, I don't see any reason why this system should not be given a try. If it succeeds, then the problem will be solved in an inexpensive manner. If it fails, draw comfort from the fact that it was a relatively inexpensive experiment.

It would be interesting to speculate as to how a pyramid combination works in all these cases where experimental proof can't be furnished. We can only hypothesize on the principles which make a combination work. I believe that this is how a pyramid combination functions.

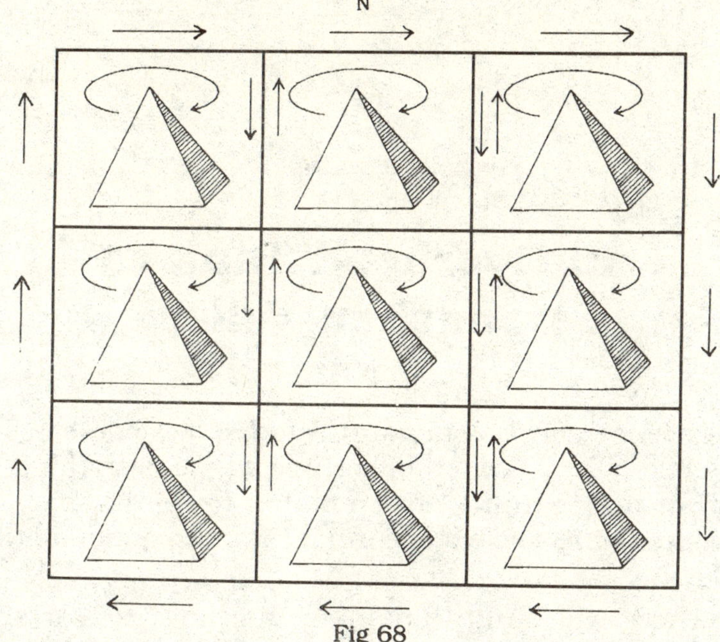

Fig 68

See the above figures. The first one shows the energy flow in individual pyramids. If you see the flow lines you will notice that in the periphery, all the flow lines move in a clockwise direction while in the center the energy line of one pyramid opposes the other. If you notice the center space between the pyramids you will find that no flow takes place due to equal and opposite forces. Thus a powerful clockwise spiral of energy lines emanate from the pyramid combination as shown in the supplements any shortfall in Vaastu energy.

For a pyramid kit containing 9 fibre glass pyramids, order has to be placed on the author. The cost of the pyramids of 9.5" base, including postage, is Rs. 4500/-

Author's address:

A.R. Hari
No. 73, 27th Cross, 11th Main,
BSK Second Stage, Bangalore - 560070

9

An Overhead Tank to Strengthen Vaastu

No science can be stagnant; neither a stage can be reached in any branch of science where everything is known and nothing else remains to be discovered. Vaastu, being a science, cannot be an exception to the rule.

There will be little point in harping back to the ancient texts for solutions to all modern-day problems. That everything is contained in the ancient books is a delusion. The structures as we know today, the various uses for which they are put into, the proliferation of skyscrappers, the severe limitations on structural corrections especially in flats, the prohibitive costs of such corrections as well as the building byelaws which appear to be exactly the opposite to the Vaastu tenets, make it imperative to expand the scope of science to encompass innovative techniques for overcoming Vaastu defects.

For any technique to be proved infallible, extensive experimental studies are essential. Apart from the time factor, enough interested owners who are willing to cooperate in such experiments are necessary. It is not that easy to find them. Further, in any experiment the attitude to accept failure without losing one's composure is an absolute must.

Under these oppressive limitations, I have carried out certain experiments and I would like to share the knowledge thus gained with you. Obviously in view of what I have stated earlier, my studies are by no means exhaustive. Conducted by a single individual over any length of time, it can never become exhaustive enough. But your cooperation and a curious mind willing to experiment can, in the long run, prove the techniques.

While suggesting these techniques for adoption. I have kept in mind the cost factor and the possibility of a total failure. Even if this were to happen, in terms of cost it will not strain you much.

What is more important is a feedback. After trying out the experiment if you can take pains to inform me in writing your experiences then perhaps your testimony will help spread the effectiveness far and wide. Irrespective of the outcome of any experiment there is always an excitement and pleasure in doing it. So put on your coat and let us enter the laboratory which may be your house or may be the one you are building for a client.

An overhead water tank is a must for every house or factory for ensuring constant supply of water.

Normally these tanks are built either from bricks or from cement (properly reinforced) in rectangular or square shape. Cylindrical and spherical tanks made from plastics are also available in the market.

While all these designs do serve as storing reservoirs, they do not bring about any change in the quality of water.

That water can be charged is an acknowledged factor. Magnetized water is a favorite method of treatment for treating both plants and human beings affected with diseases. Similarly water kept in a pyramid gets charged with cosmic energy and is reported to provide relief to some disorders.

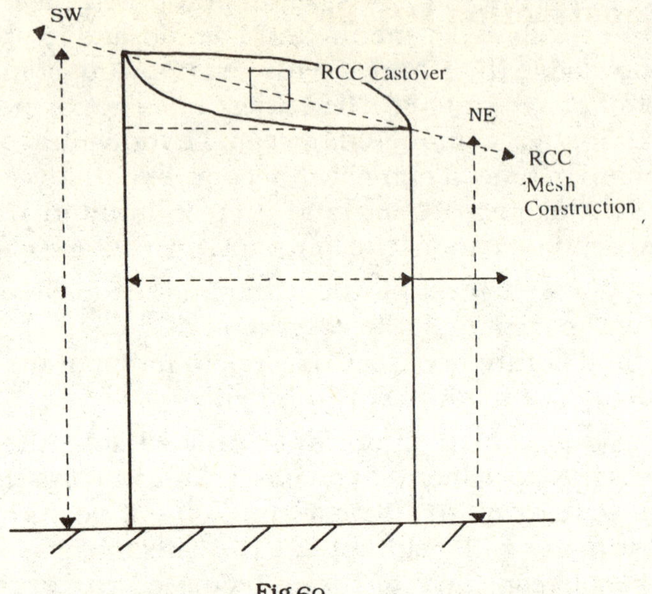

Fig 69

Note : The dotted line is the axis. Use a compass to align the tank on Southwest-Northeast Axis so that Southwest is at the Southwest corner of the building.

The overhead tank shown above, I have found from my experiments, has the quality of energizing stored water. The tank must be circular in shape and should be built from reinforced concrete cement. The length of 'b' should be so designed that an angle of 23½ degrees is formed at the top. Align the tank by using a compass on southwest-northwest so that the southwest part of the tank lies on the southwest corner of the roof. I have found that the tank gives complete relief to patients suffering form arthritis joint pains, backaches etc., especially if they sleep in the southwest bedroom over which the tank is kept. The tank can be of any size to suit your requirements. All that is required is that the RCA cover should be cast at an angle of 23½ degrees.

For best results keep the diameter and the height at northeast corner of the tank the same

Construction Details

If you are going to build the tank with the help of masons only, then these guidelines will be useful.

1. Select the southwest corner of the roof where the walls from the west and the south meet.

2. Select the size of the tank required by using the following table

Capacity in Litres	Diameter of the Tank (Inside)
785	1 mt
2650	1.5 mt
6280	2 mt

For example, if the height at the northeast is one meter then the height at the southwest of the tank (not of your building) will be 1.4348 times the diameter.

After selecting the tank of the required capacity, build the tank to have the same height all round on the platform at southwest corner of your building. Ensure that the reinforcement rods are long and project out to the maximum height at southwest.

Thus after building the tank of the required capacity you would reach the first stage, where you have a cylindrical tank with rods projecting out.

Now with the help of a compass determine the exact southwest corner of the tank and mark the northeast and southwest points on the tank with the help of a colored pencil.

Keeping the rod at the southwest point at 1.4348 times the diameter, cut the remaining rods progressively so that at the northeast corner there is no projecting rod. Now you can continue with the meshwork and the cement plastering of the projected portion and then give the finishing touches to the talk.

The roof of the tank is to be cast in the same inclined manner with a central opening for an inspection cover.

The cover can be metallic which is a standard item available in the market.

You now have an overhead water tank which has an inclined top which exactly corresponds to the way the earth is inclined. Store the water and use it as you would do in case of other tanks. However do not forget to record your observations for the rent six months after the installation of the water tank. Apart from the benefits which I have mentioned earlier and which were based on my observations, I have a gut feeling that the tank can reduce the ill-effects of defective Vaastu. Fig 69.

As I have explained in the earlier chapters we are dealing with an energy field in a structure here. We want the flow to take place from the northeast to the southwest. This can be achieved in two ways. Either increase the intensity of forces in the northeast or reduce the negativity in the southwest.

The first alternative may not be available at all where the structure is at defective northeast. If northeast correction is impossible, then the only scientific way of looking at an alternative method is to decrease the negativity in the southwest.

10

Measuring a Vaastu Field

Can we measure the strength of a Vaastu field? This is a question which is being raised by several people and needs a satisfactory answer.

While all physical matter or forces can be quantified and measured, here we do not actually know what is the nature of energy we are talking about when we talk of Vaastu. I have heard that the Bovis meter and Lecher antenna can be used to measure the energy in a structure.

It is necessary to examine these instruments from the point of view of Vaastu. No doubt these instruments which were devised decades back measure some characteristic of a structure when placed inside it. No doubt it gives different measurements in each structure. But does this reflect the strength of the Vaastu field? Is it not more than possible that they pick up one parameter out of several which could only be misleading?

For example the Bovis units for some of the items are as under:-

Human Being — 6500 Bovis

Chakras — 6500 to 16000 Bovis

Church Bell — 11000 Bovis

Tibetan Temple — 14000 Bovis

Swastika (Any Size) — 1000000 Bovis

You will find that the above comparison is between an animate thing like a person and inanimate things like Chakras, Church bell, etc. It is clear that we are just comparing one component which is common for all the above mentioned items but there necessarily every similarity ends.

Take an example. I have a weighing scale and I take the weight of ten individuals. No doubt I have measured one component i.e., the weight, out of several hundred components of which the particular individuals are made of. But if I were to qualify the individuals on the basis of the weight, would it be correct?

The weight component is just one parameter. It cannot tell me, for example, the age of the individual, sex, height, complexion, health status, nature, qualification or intellectual abilities of the individuals. If I come to the conclusion that higher the weight better is the person, I am totally wrong because in the absence of the rest of the parameters I cannot arrive at a conclusion regarding the individual. Thus here we have an instrument which reads one parameter of the different individuals, but does not give a complete picture of any individual.

More or less we have the same problem with the Bovis units and the Lecher antenna. To measure anything you have to first know whether it is a single entity or a combination of several. Thereafter we have to identify each entity and establish a unit.

As far as Vaastu energy is concerned, which we can also call bioenergy present in a structure, we are not aware of the components. We know it exists. We can feel it when we are in a high energy field. We feel peaceful, calm and relaxed. Go to a structure which does not follow the tenets of Vaastu and you will feel gloomy and depressed. Every structure has a subtle atmosphere which is unique to it, but we do not know for certain what it is.

We know it affects the way we think, the way we interact with others and the way we look at life. But if asked to explain, we have to throw up our hands helplessly.

Because we are dealing with a subtle force, any form of measurement becomes difficult. When I incorporated certain corrections in a house, the owner remarked after a few days "Mr. Hari, it is not that the problems have disappeared, but I am no longer tense. I am fully relaxed and cheerful. I feel more in a position to tackle the problems than I ever was" How do we quantify such feelings?

It has always been difficult to quantify anything that depends on one's mental state. While we can measure the height, weight, pulse and blood pressure of individuals, we have no gadgets to measure anger, hatred, happiness, jealousy, etc. Human emotions are beyond the scope of every science as it cannot be measured, evaluated or compared.

The problem is that this world of emotions, which operates only at the mental level, matters to us much more than the physical one. Our feelings, our joys and sorrows, our likes and dislikes, our elations and depressions, our hopes and worries are the ones which are more important to us than the physical self.

While one can accept that bioenergy exists and that the body has to continuously replenish it from the outside sources, it is almost impossible to determine what constitutes bioenergy or how much of it is present in a healthy body or how much of it is lacking in a diseased person. If we can have this information then there will be no disease which cannot be cured. Thus any instruments if it has to be taken seriously will have to be capable of measuring the bioenergy not only that is present in a structure but of every human, plant and animal as well. If this could be achieved, then we would truly achieve ultimate knowledge.

Under these circumstances, it would be a folly to depend on instruments to pick up and measure Vaastu fields. We have to recognise and accept that bioenergy is too subtle a force to measure. At least as of now we have no device to measure it.

Thus whenever we effect a correction, the only way of determining whether the additional field supplied has compensated the shortfall is to wait and watch. If the desired results come through, then the field supplied is adequate. If not, further efforts to supplement the field become necessary.

Bhrigu Samhita

—Dr T.M. Rao

Bhrigu Samhita is an astrological classic written by Maharishi Bhrigu in the Vedic Period. This was the first treatise on predictive astrology which formed the basis for further research and analysis. This book is a concise version of the original Bhrigu Samhita. It is specially written to cater to the needs and interests of both laymen and experts. It provides valuable hints on how to find out the character of a native, his moral inclination, and his fortunes and misfortunes in various walks of life. It also imparts useful information with regard to longevity and prosperity of the native, his parents, brothers and children. Self-explanatory content well-segregated into various chapters would enable not only a professional astrologer, but also an amateur to predict with accuracy the future of the native and form an opinion as to how a planet is disposed in a particular nativity.

Many of the books available on predictive astrology are neither easy enough to be understood by the general public nor fully satisfactory for the pundits. Therefore the primary view kept in this book is that because the mystery of the whole human life is hidden in the nine planets of a horoscope, it will not be possible to discuss the events of the whole life of the native till the effects of every planet is not clearly known. Without it, the complicated science of astrology cannot be simplified.

Demy Size • Pages: 310
Price: Rs. 250/- • Postage: Rs. 25/-

More Books on
Astrology/Vastu/Hypnotism

CATALOGUE 2016

J-3/16, Daryaganj, New Delhi-110002
Ph.: 23276539, 23272783-84, Fax: 011-23260518

FREE Tutorial CD

Available in Marathi, Tamil, Telugu, Punjabi also.

Big Size 18.5 x 24 cm
Pages over 392 0004 R

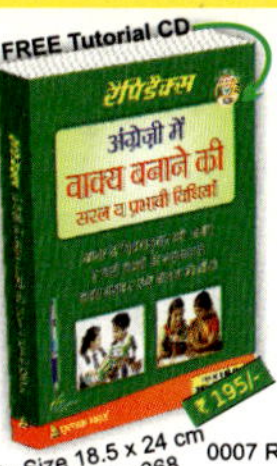

Big Size 18.5 x 24 cm
Pages over 264
8722 F

FREE Tutorial CD

Big Size 18.5 x 24 cm
Pages over 368 0007 R

FREE Tutorial DVD

Available in Tamil, Telugu also

Big Size 18.5 x 24 cm
Pages 384 0001 R

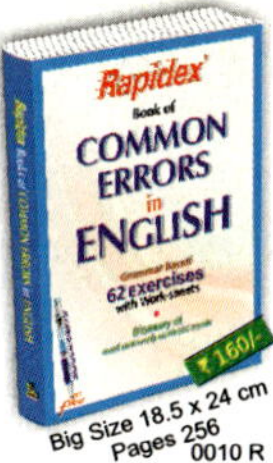

Big Size 18.5 x 24 cm
Pages 360
0014 R

Rapidex Book of COMMON ERRORS in ENGLISH
₹ 160/-

Big Size 18.5 x 24 cm
Pages 256
0010 R

FREE Tutorial CD

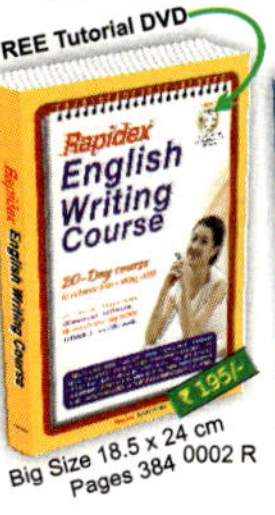

₹ 215/-

112 S
0008 R

Big Size 18.5 x 24 cm
Pages 388

FREE Tutorial DVD

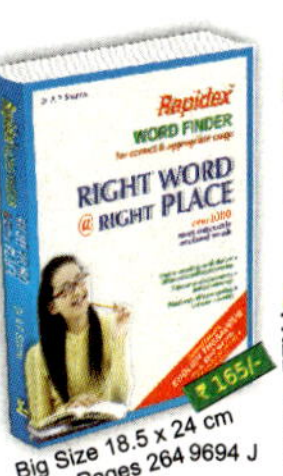

Big Size 18.5 x 24 cm
Pages 384 0002 R

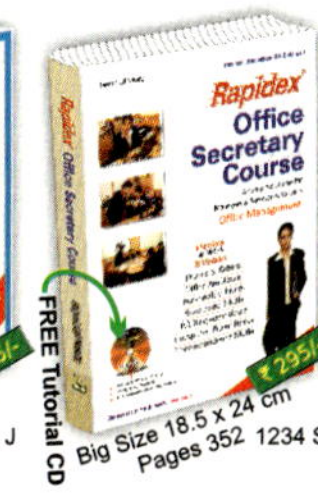

Big Size 18.5 x 24 cm
Pages 264 9694 J

FREE Tutorial CD

Rapidex Office Secretary Course
₹ 295/-

Big Size 18.5 x 24 cm
Pages 352 1234 S

With a CD for learning correct pronunciation of English and other language

Big Size 250 Pages & above in each

A 14-Volume series teaching 6 Regional Languages through Hindi & vice versa

1232 A - Assamese-Hindi
1233 B - Hindi-Assamese
1215 S - Hindi-Tamil
1217 S - Hindi-Telugu
1218 S - Hindi-Bangla
1219 S - Hindi-Gujarati
1216 S - Hindi Kannada
1236 A - Malayalam-Arabic
1221 S - Tamil-Hindi
1223 S - Telugu-Hindi
1224 S - Bangla-Hindi
1225 S - Gujarati-Hindi
1222 S - Kannada-Hindi
1128 B - Hindi-Arabic
1220 S - Malayalam-Hindi
1214 S - Hindi-Malayalam

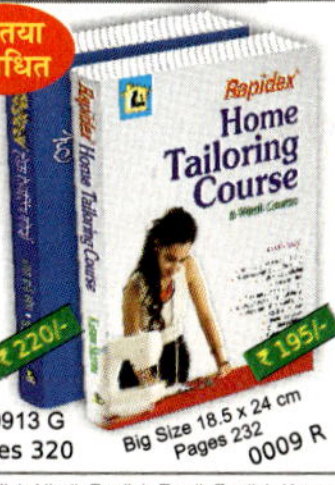

9913 G
ges 320

Big Size 18.5 x 24 cm
Pages 232
0009 R

9742 C Size 13.5 x 19.5 cm
Pages 464

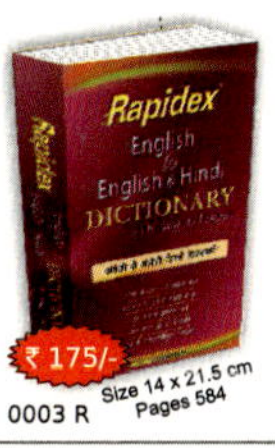

0003 R Size 14 x 21.5 cm
Pages 584

FREE Tutorial CD

9661 M Size 13.5 x 19.5 cm
Pages 576

Pages 252-256 in each

6611 G - English – Hindi
1133 A - English – Bangla
1132 D - English – Tamil
1134 B - English – Kannada
1136 D - English – Telugu
1137 A - English – Gujarati
1135 C - English – Malayalam

Rapidex Dictionary of Spoken Words
98/- each

Over 1200 entries with coloured pictures

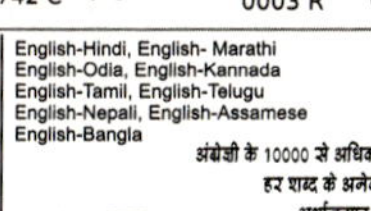

अंग्रेज़ी के 10000 से अधिक शब्द
हर शब्द के अनेक अर्थ
अर्थानुसार प्रयोग

English-Hindi, English-Marathi,
English-Odia, English-Kannada,
English-Tamil, English-Telugu,
English-Nepali, English-Bangla
English to Punjabi & Hindi,
English-Assamese

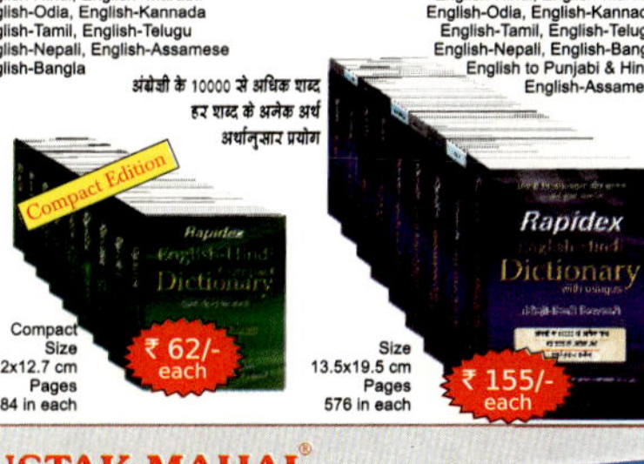

Compact Size 10.2x12.7 cm
Pages 384 in each

Size 13.5x19.5 cm
Pages 576 in each

6607 L

POPULAR SCIENCE

NEW RELEASES

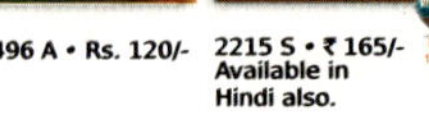

9496 A • Rs. 120/-

2215 S • ₹ 165/- Available in Hindi also. Contains: 10 Projects

2214 S • ₹ 165/- Available in Hindi also. FREE Tutorial CD

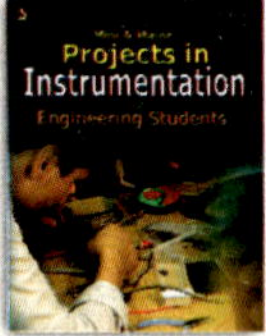

8716 T • ₹ 160/-

8733 D • ₹ 195/-

9660 K • ₹ 295/-

8702 B • ₹ 150/-

6678 D • ₹ 195/-

6679 A • ₹ 150/-

8767 C • Rs. 120/-

0019 R • Rs. 160/-

8762 P • Rs. 140/-

8764 T • Rs. 160/-

- Over 900 Illustrations
- Over 800 Pages
- 890 Articles
- Four Volumes

FREE Buy all 4 Vols. & get 5th Volume free with an Audio-Video DVD worth ₹ 135/-

Set 4 Vols.: ₹ 780/-
Each Vol.: ₹ 195/-

Available in Hindi & English both

This Library is must for every student *of a* School *or* a College

Also equally useful for everyone else

Price: ₹ 600/-
Contains 4 books of ₹ 150/- each

₹ 150/- Page 256 (with CD) English Conversation

₹ 150/- Page 310 Grammar & Punctuation

₹ 150/- Page 318 How to use English

₹ 150/- Page 344 English Vocabulary

4 Books of the Library

QUIZ BOOKS

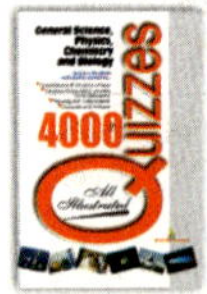

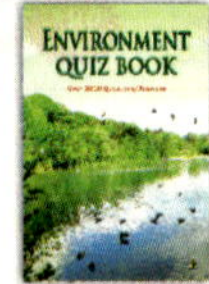

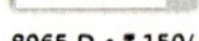

8965 D • ₹ 150/-

7726 K • ₹ 120/-

7727 L • ₹ 120/-

7723 F • ₹ 100/-

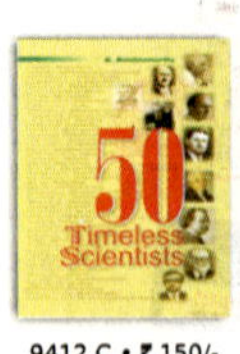

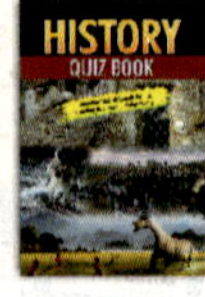

9412 C • ₹ 150/-

7753 G • ₹ 120/-

7725 B • ₹ 100/-

7722 E • ₹ 120/-

Miscellaneous

9497 B • ₹ 120/-

9783 H • ₹ 150/-

9680 B • ₹ 295/-

9686 H • ₹ 120/

SELF-IMPROVEMENT

New

9698 R • ₹ 195/- 9498 C • ₹ 180/- 9490 H • ₹ 175/- 9464 R • ₹ 80/- 9096 B • ₹ 150/- 5614 E • ₹ 150/- 4008 J • ₹ 150/- 9026 D • ₹ 120/- 9786 M • ₹ 195/-

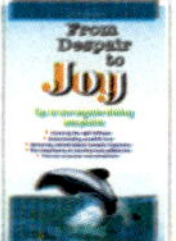

9491 J • ₹ 100/- 8885 D • ₹ 150/- 9081 D • ₹ 150/- 9091 B • ₹ 120/- 9060 B • ₹ 195/- 9684 F • ₹ 195/- 8928 D • ₹ 80/- 9449 A • ₹ 195/- 9788 R • ₹ 195/-

MANAGEMENT/JOB/CARRIER/BUSINESS & PROFESSION

All Time Bestsellers

9461 K • ₹ 150/- 5338 A • ₹ 135/- (with CD) 8979 A • ₹ 135/- 9406 B • ₹ 150/- 9672 G • ₹ 150/- 9682 D • ₹ 120/- 8729 T • ₹ 120/-

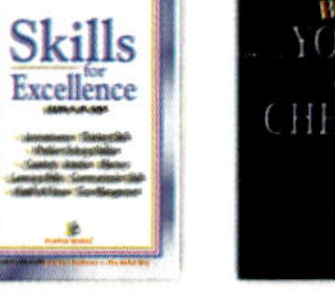

9697 P • ₹ 195/- 9313 D • ₹ 150/- 5623 B • ₹ 250/- 9439 L • ₹ 150/- 5441 D • ₹ 195/- 8883 D • ₹ 150/- 8735 F • ₹ 150/-

4018 D • ₹ 150/- 9079 B • ₹ 195/- 4005 E • ₹ 195/- 5643 B • ₹ 120/- 9431 C • ₹ 175/- 8990 C • ₹ 96/- 9763 P • Rs. 195/-

5618 D • ₹ 120/- 5640 C • ₹ 120/- 5615 D • ₹ 150/- 8972 C • ₹ 80/- 4001 A • ₹ 150/- 5646 A • ₹ 225/- 4017 D • ₹ 150/-

4 PERSONALITY DEVELOPMENT

8748 E • ₹ 195/- 9666 A • ₹ 150/- 9678 R • ₹ 195/-

9670 E • ₹ 240/- 9696 M • ₹ 220/- 9070 B • ₹ 195/-

9028 D • ₹ 175/- 5641 A • ₹ 150/- 9450 B • ₹ 195/-

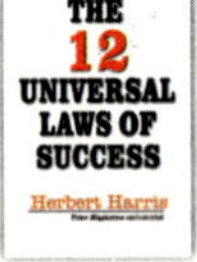

9088 C • ₹ 195/- 9667 B • ₹ 150/- 8966 E • ₹ 100/-

5639 B • ₹ 80/- 9466 T • ₹ 96/- 9973 B • ₹ 110/-

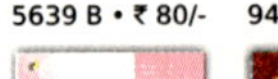

9981 B • ₹ 96/- 8868 D • ₹ 120/- 9487 E • ₹ 150/-

STUDENT DEVELOPMENT

9090 A • ₹ 220/- 9668 C • ₹ 150/- 9071 D • ₹ 165/- 8731 B • ₹ 100/- 9495 R • ₹ 175/-

9455 C • ₹ 150/- 5622 A • ₹ 120/- 9967 C • ₹ 120/-

2241 J • ₹ 100/- 94441 S • ₹ 195/- 9654 D • ₹ 100/-

9652 D • ₹ 120/- 8962 A • ₹ 150/- 9089 D • ₹ 135/-

4016 D • ₹ 160/- 4009 K • ₹ 150/- 8997 B • ₹ 120/-

4010 L • ₹ 100/- 9787 P • ₹ 100/- 2244 D • ₹ 80/-

PARENTING

9906 J • ₹ 250/- (HB) 8261 D • ₹ 180

9674 J • ₹ 220/- 9784 J • ₹ 150,

9594 K • ₹ 80/- 8917 D • ₹ 120

9458 G • ₹ 80/- 9438 B • ₹ 150

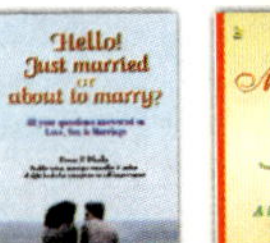

9065 A • ₹ 80/- 9994 E • ₹ 120

ALTERNATIVE THERAPIES

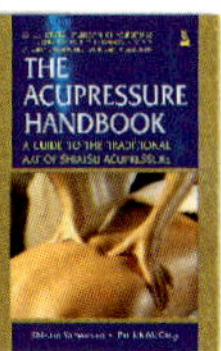

8882 F • ₹ 215/-

8983 E • ₹ 100/-

8836 D • ₹ 135/-

9935 F • ₹ 120/-

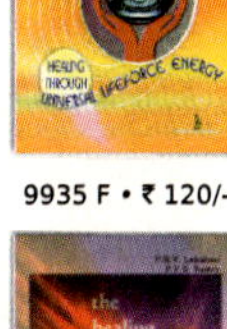

5637 D • ₹ 96/-

8889 D • ₹ 100/-

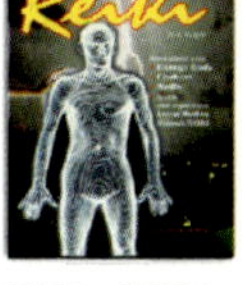

8842 D • ₹ 100/-

8941 A • ₹ 100/-

GENERAL HEALTH

9075 C • ₹ 225/-

8747 D • ₹ 150/-

9940 D • ₹ 150/-

8859 G • ₹ 80/-

8877 A • ₹ 150/-

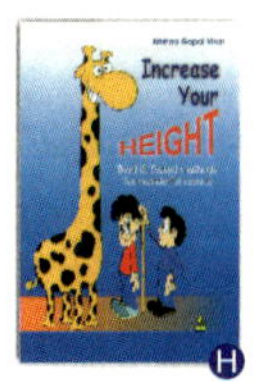

8847 M • ₹ 100/-

8870 D • ₹ 100/-

9950 B • ₹ 120/-

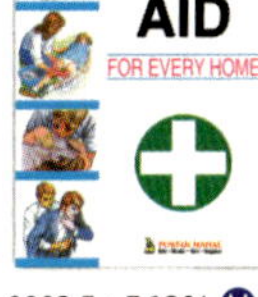

9902 F • ₹ 120/-

COMMON AILMENTS & DISEASES

8891 D • ₹ 120/-

8281 A • ₹ 100/-

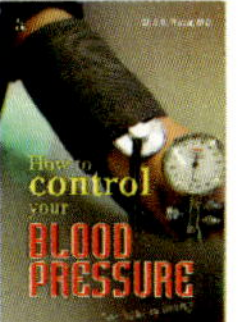

8094 D • ₹ 120/-

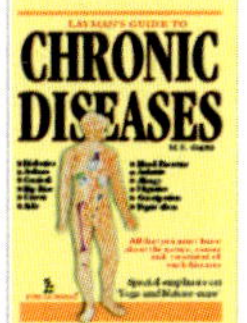

8848 D • ₹ 150/-

8276 A • ₹ 96/-

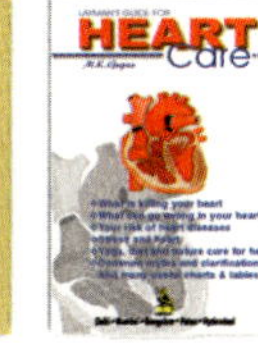

8888 D • ₹ 96/-

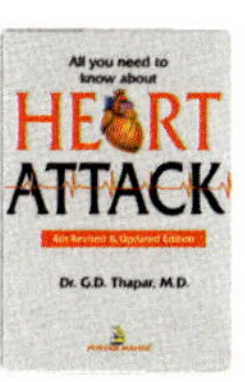

8908 D • ₹ 120/-

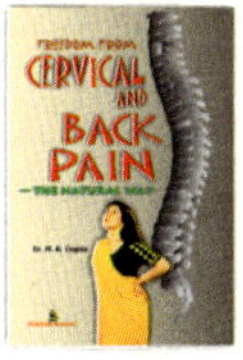

8878 B • ₹ 80/-

SLIMMING & FITNESS

8277 B • ₹ 120/-

8875 K • ₹ 120/-

9445 A • ₹ 150/-

DIET & NUTRITION

9941 D • ₹ 100/-

8904 D • ₹ 150/-

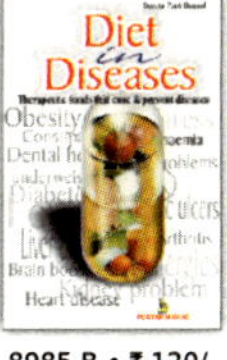

8985 B • ₹ 120/-

8968 G • ₹ 120/-

8271 C • ₹ 96/-

9037 D • ₹ 150/-

9873 C • ₹ 60/-

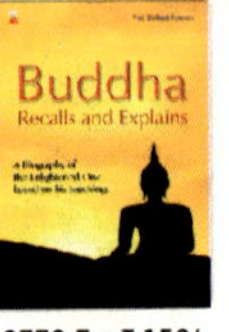

9770 E • ₹ 150/-

9453 A • ₹ 250/-

4179 A • ₹ 295/- (HB)

4138 B Rs. 250

4177 B • ₹ 250/-

9997 C • ₹ 80/-

4181 C • ₹ 195/-

9984 E • ₹ 399/- (HB)

4130 B • ₹ 120/-

9811 P • ₹ 120/-

9585 A • ₹ 96/-

9508 D • ₹ 95/-

9989 D • ₹ 96/-

4183 A • ₹ 350/- (HB)

9504 D • ₹ 100/-

9540 D • ₹ 150/-

9513 A • ₹ 195/-

4126 B • ₹ 96/-

9812 R • ₹ 120/-

9504 D • ₹ 100/-

4124 A • ₹ 120/-

4190 C • ₹ 160/-

9509 A • ₹ 150/-

4152 B • ₹ 96/-

4188 A • ₹ 160/-

4132 D • ₹ 100/-

9987 E • ₹ 150/-

9520 D • ₹ 120/-

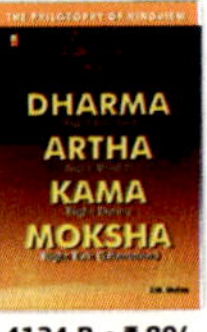

4134 B • ₹ 80/-

4182 D • ₹ 96/-

9405 A • ₹ 1

COMPUTERS

7712 K • ₹ 165/-

7711 J • ₹ 12

9768 C • ₹ 175/-

7766 A • ₹ 12

HOME MAKING / GRILLS & RAILIN

3111 E • ₹ 175/-

3107 F • ₹ 8

3106 E • ₹ 100/-

3105 D • ₹ 1(

3108 G • ₹ 150/-

3104 M • ₹ 1

ASTROLOGY/VASTU/HYPNOTISM/PAMISTRY

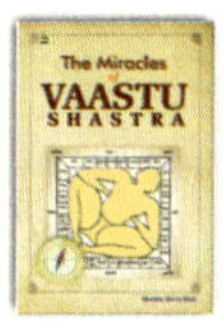

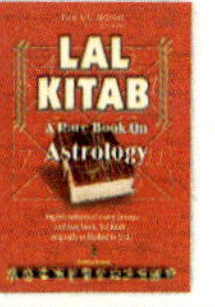

9871 A • ₹ 240/- 9693 H • ₹ 195/- 9671 F • ₹ 195/- 2127 D • ₹ 250/- 4177 C • ₹ 295/- 9086 A • ₹ 295/-HB

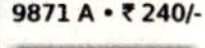

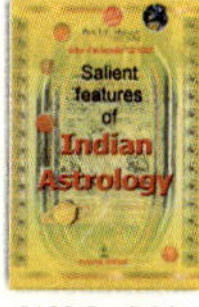

2116 D • ₹ 150/- 8259 D • ₹ 88/- 2109 F • ₹ 150/- 2112 D • ₹ 120/- 3110 B • ₹ 120/- 2133 B • ₹ 96/-

8899 D • ₹ 195/- 8925 D • ₹ 96/- 2132 A • ₹ 150/- 9432 D • ₹ 150/- 2120 D • ₹ 150/- 2109 F • ₹ 100/-

ENGLISH IMPROVEMENT

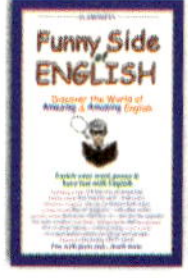

7540 D • ₹ 175/- 5541 C • ₹ 196/- 6651 E • ₹ 195/- 9448 D • ₹ 175/- 9056 A • ₹ 125/- 5538 D • ₹ 100/-

PERSON & PERSONALITIES

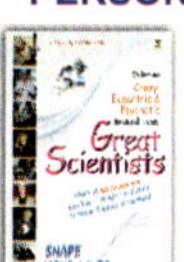

9669 D • ₹ 120/- 9825 E • ₹ 150/- 2113 D • ₹ 195/- 9764 R • ₹ 100/- 8991 D • ₹ 120/-

BODY/BEAUTY CARE

8093 D • ₹ 150/- 9986 B • ₹ 150/- 8971 B • ₹ 120/- 9922 F • ₹ 120/- 8865 F • ₹ 120/-

JOKES HUMOUR & SATIRE

2342 C • ₹ 100/- 2343 D • ₹ 100/-

2341 B • ₹ 96/- 2318 A • ₹ 96/-

2330 B • ₹ 96/- 2319 B • ₹ 96/-

FICTION

Set Code SH 001

Set Code 9795 A

Set Code 9752 B • ₹ 550/-

SAYING/QUOTATIONS/PROVERBS

9474 F • ₹ 170/- 9789 A • ₹ 150/- 8999 D • ₹ 80/-

9953 A • ₹ 100/- 8947 E • ₹ 100/- 8890 D • ₹ 150/-

5512 A • ₹ 150/- 8963 B • ₹ 80/- 9425 A • ₹ 60/-

FUN, FACTS, MAGIC & MYSTERIES

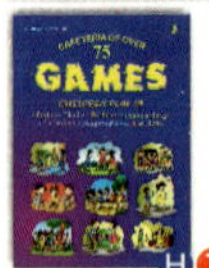
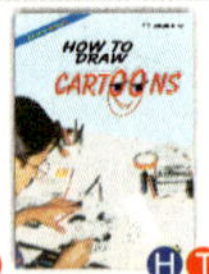

9484 B • ₹ 150/- 2275 D • ₹ 120/- 9479 M • ₹. 120/- 9470 B • ₹ 100/-

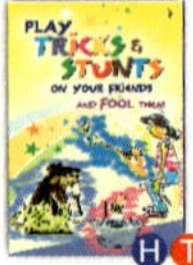

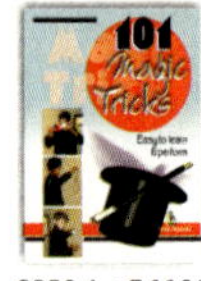

2208 M • ₹ 100/- 9816 D • ₹ 100/- 2247 F • ₹ 100/- 2250 A • ₹ 110/-

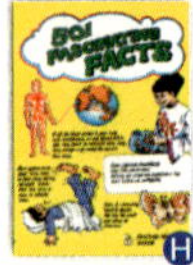

2211 F • ₹ 100/- 9457 E • ₹ 150/- 2237 M • ₹ 100/- 2335 A • ₹ 80/-

2243 L • ₹ 100/- 9775 M • ₹ 100/- 9985 A • ₹ 80/- 5110 A • ₹ 80/-

2337 C • ₹ 100/- 2336 B • ₹ 100/- 2331 C • ₹ 100/- 9977 B • ₹ 100/-

YOGA & MEDITATION

8269 A • ₹ 195/- 9998 D • ₹ 150/- 8939 D • ₹ 96/-

9958 S • ₹ 160/- 9087 B • ₹ 195/- 2118 F • ₹ 120/-

8901 D • ₹ 150/- 8099 D • ₹ 80/- 9025 D • ₹ 80/-

HOMEOPATHY, AYURDEDA

9446 B • ₹ 150/- 8887 D • ₹ 195/- 8270 B • ₹ 195/- 8923 D • ₹ 195/-

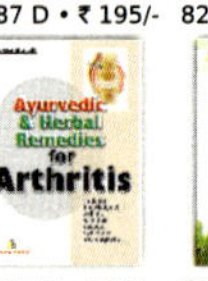

8010 D • ₹ 96/- 9094 E • ₹ 96/- 8944 D • ₹ 175/- 8948 A • ₹ 120/-

WORLD FAMOUS SERIES

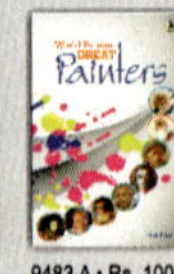

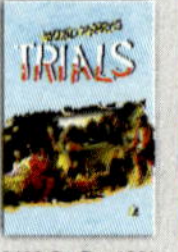

9472 D • ₹ 100/- 5164 E • ₹ 100/- 9483 A • Rs. 100/- 51107 • ₹ 100/- 9766 A • Rs. 100/- 9489 G • Rs. 100/- 9761 M • Rs. 120/-

World Famous Mysterious Objects
True Stories of Mowglis and other Wild Childrens
World Famous Treasures (Lost and Found)
World Famous WARs & Battles
True Stories of Mystic Places
World Famous Adventures
World Famous Military Operations
World Famous Spy Scandals
World Famous Spies & Spymasters
World Famous Crooks & Con Men
True Stories 81 Weird Humans
True Stories of Great Explorers
World Famous Strange Mysteries
and many more.......

LOVE, ROMANCE & SEX

9602 B • Rs. 125/- 8260 D • Rs. 96/- 8266 D • Rs. 80/- 8278 C • Rs. 100/- 8916 D • Rs. 120/-

MORAL, WISDOM & FAIRY TALES

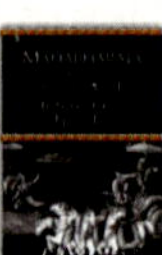

9677 P • Rs. 150/- 9486 D • Rs. 250/- 8967 F • Rs. 80/- 9077 E • Rs.120/- 9563 N • Rs. 125/- 2289 D • ₹